Peggy Cole's

COUNTRY COTTAGE COMPANION

Oh, Adam was a Gardener
And God who made him sees,
That half a proper Gardener's work
Is done upon his knees.
So when your work is finished
You can wash your hands and pray
For the Glory of the Garden
That it may not pass away.

Rudyard Kipling

Peggy Cole's
COUNTRY COTTAGE COMPANION

Best Wishes
Peggy Cole

DAVID & CHARLES
Newton Abbot London North Pomfret (Vt)

For My Grandchildren

ACKNOWLEDGEMENTS

Many thanks to my dear friend, Iris Stebbings, without whose immense patience and ability to decipher my original notes, the compilation of this book would not have been possible.

My thanks are due also to Alfred Geary for his superb drawings, to Seley Little for his helpful advice, to Olive Cass, MBE, for her admirable snippets and to Beth Chatto for finding time to write the foreword to this book and thanks to Readers Digest, Dr D. G. Hessayon, PBI Books, and John Seymour, Gardeners Delight

British Library Cataloguing in Publication Data

Cole, Peggy
Peggy Cole's country cottage companion
1. Country gardens. Cultivation
I. Title
635

ISBN 0-7153-9119-4

Phototypeset by ABM Typographics Ltd Hull
and printed in Great Britain by
Redwood Burn Ltd Trowbridge
for David & Charles Publishers plc
Brunel House Newton Abbot Devon

Published in the United States of America
by David & Charles Inc
North Pomfret Vermont 05053 USA

Contents

VISIT AN ENGLISH GARDEN
KNOWN AS
AKENFIELD
1, PARK LANE
CHARSFIELD, SUFFOLK
(ON B1078)
OPEN TO THE PUBLIC
FROM
MAY TO SEPTEMBER
2.30 pm to 7.00 pm DAILY
MANY UNUSUAL FLOWERS,
VEGETABLES, GREENHOUSES
AS SHOWN ON TV 'GARDENERS WORLD'
AUGUST 1983
PROCEEDS FOR CHARITIES

Foreword

I am delighted to be asked by Peggy Cole to write a foreword to her second book. The joy of this book, and her first, *A Country Girl At Heart,* is that they are as fresh and sweet-smelling as newly baked bread. Reading them I will be always reminded of a fine summer morning when one of my brothers took me to see her garden. I was unprepared for the transformation of a bare rectangle of Suffolk soil into a garden blissfully unaware of such limitations.

From the brilliantly bedded entrance, through a little courtyard dripping with flowers, between quiet shaded borders full of green things, to the superbly kept vegetable garden complete with a pen of chuckling hens – it was a delight. But not more so than Peggy, with her quiet, calm presence, her soft, gentle speech. For those who cannot meet her, or see her garden, and for all whose interests lie in natural things, this book brings the art of genuine country living, distilled from many lifetimes but rarely brought together in one person. It is crammed with commonsense and sound practice, of facts, fancies, and fun, but above all it shows how rich life can be, lived close to the soil.

Peggy's achievements have become famous, rightly so, but she herself remains untouched since she never sought fame, but simply followed the inclinations of a wise and generous spirit.

Beth Chatto

Beth Chatto
Elmstead Market

Introduction

My aim with this book is to follow up the story of my rural upbringing, my married-life 'on the land' and my subsequent adventures which I told in *A Country Girl At Heart,* with a complimentary practical guide to traditional, country-style gardening. What follows is not a comprehensive textbook on the subject, (many excellent examples exist already) but a fairly informal guide, based upon my own experience in developing and maintaining my widely-known 'patch' in the heart of the Suffolk countryside.

Readers of the earlier book – and many of my summer visitors – will know how I started the garden with my late husband, Ernie, in 1970 and how, as a result of our becoming involved in the film of Ronald Blythe's wonderful book, *Akenfield,* we caught the attention of the media and a wide public. Nowadays my dear brother, Ronnie, helps me with much of the practical work round the year, but I still do the planting and coaxing and training of all the plants, along with many other activities which have all grown out of this beloved plot of Suffolk soil.

A Country Girl At Heart was mainly concerned with my family life in typical Suffolk villages over the past fifty years, but it also included sections on the garden, the film, the honour and excitement of the private visit by HRH Princess Margaret to my garden in 1984 and that most popular event in the country calendar – the Summer Show. There were also recipes for cakes, puddings, wines and jams among other delicious temptations – and tips for winning those coveted show prizes.

Living close to the soil and the seasons – natural blessings which so many other people today can only enjoy occasionally and city-dwellers hardly at all – I feel specially glad to be able to share the joys of my garden with my visitors, my radio audiences and now, once again, my readers.

Country life today changes in step with the rapid changes in urban living, but happily those of us with our own gardens, whether small or large, have a relationship with nature that is, basically, unchanging; our gardens are still there to be loved and tended in the age-old ways of our forebears, oases of peace and harmony in a world of widespread discord and strife.

Country lore is a continuing process, like any other, and all the ideas and practices in this book stem from methods handed down to me by my grandfather, my father and my late husband, modified of course by the continual up-dating of theory, techniques and products, which I study and try out in the course of my year-to-year work in the garden.

Truly

One is nearer to God's heart in a garden,
Than anywhere else on Earth.

Peggy Cole
Charsfield, 1987

AKENFIELD GARDEN

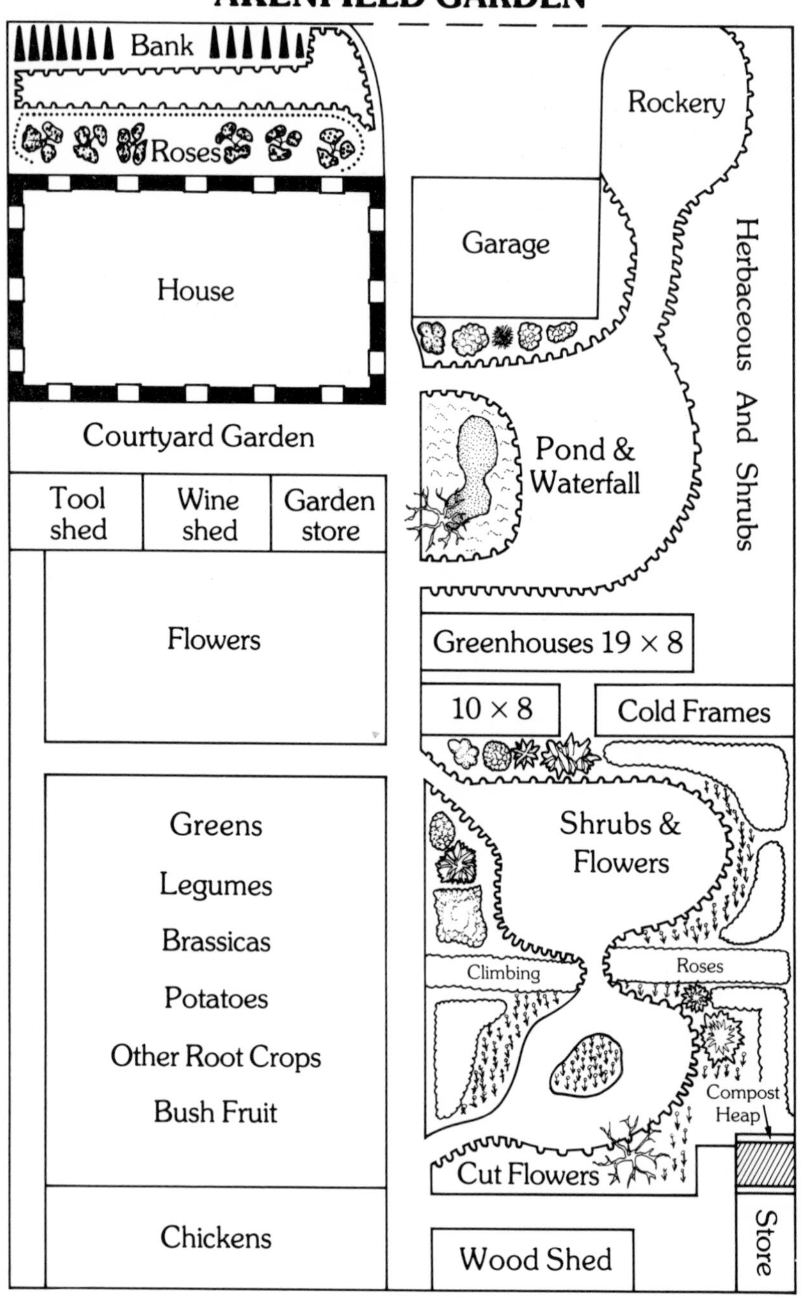

What is a Gardener?

A gardener is an artist, a navvy; part optimist and at times, part idiot.

It's easy when you know how, so they say. If you are rich and don't know how, you simply ring the nearest garden centre and write out a cheque. If you have no money but lots of friends, you can lay in a selection of tools and enlist all the free labour you can find. All the gardening books tell you that there is no short cut to gardening and that the ground must be well-prepared first.

The first spring day produces great activity from the gardener. The lethargy of the winter vanishes and out come the mower, the hedgecutters and the shears. The daffodils which can be relied on to put on a good show no matter what you do to them will bring a warmth to the heart of every gardener.

Come summer, he will be head-gardener, under-gardener and everything else in between and will be out in the garden at every opportunity. If there is a lawn, he'll be spending hours cutting, rolling, weeding and raking. (I will not elaborate at this point, on the joys of growing your own fruit and vegetables, despite the battles with the slugs, mice, birds, red spiders, greenflies and blackflies!)

Summer is the season when the weather stops being bad and becomes simply terrible. This is the time of year when the gardener needs to summon all his optimism and when he needs a sense of humour. It takes so little to make him happy – the perfume of a beautiful bloom, a plate of runner beans freshly picked or a bowl of raspberries, but he can be reduced to deepest depression if, after spending an entire evening watering his garden, he finishes half an hour before the start of a two-day downpour. Such are the things that make or break our gardener's day.

The Kiss of the Sun for pardon,
The song of the birds for Mirth,
One is nearer God's Heart in a garden,
Than anywhere else on Earth.

Poppycock! By the time the thousand and one jobs in the garden are done, or the gardener has returned from holiday to find his lettuces have bolted, the garden is a riot of colourful weeds and the birds have stuffed themselves with his choice shoots and berries, the words that spring to the lips of the average gardener would not gladden the heart of anyone.

Autumn arrives – now that's the season the gardener loves. Aside from it's obvious beauty of mists and mellow fruitfulness, he can wander about and enjoy the wonder of his garden without feeling guilty because he is not mowing the lawn. Of course, that is *early* autumn; before long, down come the leaves and then there is the back-breaking job of clearing them and generally tidying up for winter.

What is a Gardener? Why do we do it? you ask. I don't know; I only know that I couldn't do without my garden.

THROUGH THE YEAR IN MY GARDEN

January

January Warm – the Lord have Mercy

GARDENING is a never-ending joy; it is really a close look at God's creation and an enjoyment of it. One thing is certain – you can never stop learning with gardening and I always keep a diary (a five-year one is best). My last task of the day, before I lie down in my bed, is to write down jobs which I have been doing in the garden and keep a record of the weather. So, if a diary was among your Christmas presents, jot down what to sow, plant and your spraying year. Do try to keep up your notes, they will be so useful for the following year.

I am going to take you through my year in the garden, with some country cures and 'old wives' tales' included, (I believe in some of their hints, but not all).

First then, January. In the dark days it is difficult to fit in much outdoor work in the garden. However, opportunity should be taken to catch up with the last of the winter digging. My brother Ronnie likes to get all mine done by the end of December, leaving the soil in large clods. The frost will break this down and nature does the rest. If you are putting compost or farmyard manure into the soil, it is best to spread it on the land and dig it in before the hard frosts come. As soon as the frost goes, pull down the soil with a rake to make a good tilth. The topsoil must be fine if you are going to plant seeds in it. We always pull the land down with an old chrome (an implement with a long handle and long, hooked teeth for raking muck from carts, used in fields or farmyard). My soil is medium-heavy and it's no good trying to walk on my garden if it is wet. We call it 'loving' soil as it sticks to your boots!

The experts say you should manure a garden every second year, but as I can get plenty of good cow muck, we muck every year.

People ask me why my plants grow so well and I say that the answer really lies in the soil; or to put it another way, 'what you put in, you can get out'. You must not put muck on the garden where the parsnips or carrots are to be grown, as the long roots will go 'fang-ing' – they will feed on the muck instead of going down into the soil. If the soil is sandy then all the compost you give it won't get the soil right, as the rain will wash it right through. It's also the same with clay, only peat and manure will get it broken down.

There are two ways of making fertiliser to my way of thinking. One is using all the carbon matter, the tops of potatoes and cabbages, (don't put potato peelings on compost heaps as they will grow) and mixing it up with household scraps on a heap at the top of the garden. The other is the use of chemical fertilisers. In my opinion, too much artificial fertiliser is being used today. For instance, if you use too much fertiliser on your potatoes they have no flavour and do not keep very well, and when they are cooked they come up watery with big black blotches on them. I still say that you can't beat good old muck for a potato bed.

A good idea, if you have moved into a new house and don't know much about the soil, is to obtain a simple little kit to test the condition of the soil. This is particularly important where heavy ground is concerned, to see if it needs lime put on it. The most important test is for ph, which is a measure of the soil's acidity/alkalinity. For example, potatoes like fairly acid soil whereas mint (herb) likes alkaline soil, so it may need liming.

I often get asked about using soot. This is good for nitrogen, but it must be kept for a good six months before using, as it will only scorch the plants (soot can be used as a feed for leeks, made up in a bucket, with water). You must also be careful if using poultry or pig manure. If it is freshly taken from the farm it contains a good deal of ammonia and this is inclined to scorch the roots and leaves of plants. It is best made into a heap and stored at the top of the garden, out of the way, for a year.

Onion skin, very thin,
Mild winter coming in,
Onion skin thick and tough,
Coming winter cold and rough.

Another job to be getting on with, is pruning. Fruit pruning should be completed this month; the trees given their annual winter tar-oil wash treatment to clean them up for the season ahead. The golden rule is never to prune more than is necessary, to form a well-shaped tree and encourage the production of fruiting spurs. Under-pruning is better than over-pruning. I was always told that 'you should be able to throw your hat through the middle of the tree, not letting it hit the branches', meaning that you should have a nice open-centred tree. If you have a tree four–five years old, remove all dead, dying and badly placed crossing branches in winter. Also, shorten the laterals produced the previous summer, by about one-third, if it is found that only the buds near the tips tend to break in the spring. The leaders may be left unpruned if the tree is growing well. Fruit buds should then form on two-year-old wood.

I still think that the Bramley Seedling is the best cooking apple; I have only one apple tree in the garden and that is a Bramley. These apples, with a little bit of luck, will keep right through until March. My favourite dessert apple used to be a Cox Orange Pippin, but since the local fruit farmers started to grow Jonagold they have taken first place in my mind. They are a super apple, juicy and sweet, with a good rich flavour. The picking season is later than for most apples – November – and the fruit keeps well into March.

The only soft fruits which I grow are raspberries and a forty-gallon drum planted with strawberries. The raspberries are an old variety called 'Phyllis King'; the canes were given to me by an old gardener who always used to win first prize in the local flower shows with this variety. Raspberries don't need a lot doing to them, just remove the canes which have borne fruit and restrict the number of new canes to four–six per stool (or root). Tie-in to the wire framework and prune canes in early spring, to about 5– 6ft. My strawberries used to take up a lot of room, so I have home-made a strawberry barrel out of an old forty-gallon water tank.

For the amateur, gooseberries and red and white currants should be trained to grow on a short single leg, to make it easier for picking the fruit. These fruit bushes are pruned in a different way from

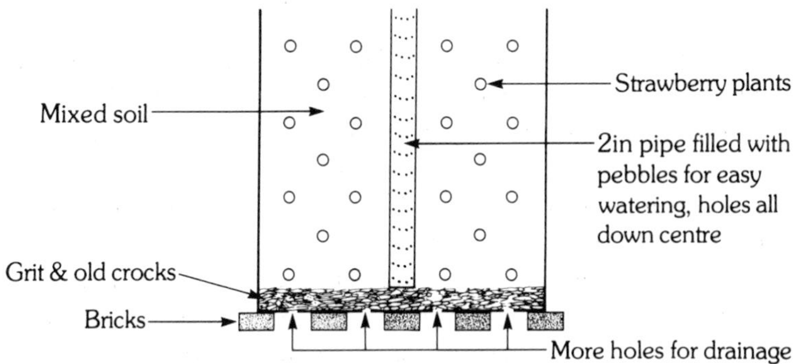

blackcurrants. In winter, cut back the growing point of each branch by half and shorten the side shoots to a node about 3–4in from the main branch. Remove any weak or diseased branches, also those crossing and growing into the centre.

Blackcurrant bushes should be pruned to ground level after planting. The first season no further pruning is necessary; then in subsequent years all fruited wood should be removed, leaving only strong, unfruited stems.

One of the most important tasks in winter, if there have been plenty of high winds and gales, is to go round the garden looking at shrubs and newly planted trees and bushes to see if there are any gaps left around the stem bases. Fill these in with your heel; if left they fill with water and neck rot sets in. If evergreens are planted in the autumn, some protection may be needed if the site is very exposed. Old sacking, polythene or even fine mesh netting wrapped around a framework of canes is adequate. Another job is to tap snow from shrubs and hedges to prevent them being broken down by sheer weight.

As the days lengthen, so the cold strengthen.
If the first snow falls on soft moist
earth, it indicates a small harvest.
But if on hard, frozen soil, there will
be a good harvest the following year.

People often forget another important thing; to get the mower and shears to the grinders. A good tip here is not to stand your mower on a concrete floor as the damp creeps up and will rust the blades. Stand it on a block of wood. Talking of rust, it's a good time to get all your garden tools and give them a good rub with an oily rag. Also at this time of year I bring in all my white, plastic garden labels and clean off the old writing with a soap pad, (a useful indoor job in bad weather).

Early January is the time to get your seed order despatched; if you leave it too late the new varieties will be sold out. It is the same with potatoes; buy them early, taking them out of the net bags and standing them in egg trays for chitting, placing them side by side with the rose end uppermost – this is the end in which most of the dormant sprouts (potato eyes) are concentrated. Keep in a coolish place, free from frost. I don't grow many potatoes; just four rows of earlies (Irish Peace, Maris Bard and Pentland Javelin) and two rows maincrop (Drayton).

If the birds begin to sing in January,
frosts are on the way out.

There is just one more outside job which we can do and that is to cover the rhubarb with an old box or bucket, turning it upside down and putting it over the rhubarb crown. If you can find a little dry straw or dry leaves, put these on the crown first. Leave it for a few weeks and you will be surprised with nice early rhubarb!

A January spring is worth nothing

In the greenhouse

One of my tips at this time of year is not to be tempted to sow bedding plants too soon as light levels are still comparatively low, especially in the greenhouse. If there are heavy snowfalls, take a soft broom and sweep snow off the roof of the greenhouse.

I use soil-less compost for sowing and re-potting, so the first job is to get a bag of compost and stand it in the greenhouse to warm up for three-four days before use. This compost has come a long way since I started to grow my own bedding plants. Years ago I had to take a bucket and walk along the hedgerows to find good loam and then mix my own compost with peat, sand and fertiliser, which would then need sterilizing. So, I have gone over to all soil-less compost, except when I mix my own to plant a few pots of chrysanthemums. I like to use perlite and vermiculite to help lighten the compost.

When sowing seeds it is best to get the trays ready the day before filling them to the top with compost and levelling off. Press the compost with the base of an empty flower pot or a flat presser. I then stand the trays in a bowl of water mixed with some Cheshunt compound, this being a fungicide; if you use a watering can, it tends to float the peat to the surface. The seeds may now be sown and covered with sifted compost. If you are using very small seeds, mix them with silver sand – I have even used flour and leave them uncovered, or press them gently into the compost. Cover the container with a sheet of clean glass or polythene and then a sheet of newspaper to exclude strong sunlight. Globules of moisture will collect on the cover and this should be turned over each day to remove the condensation. As soon as germination takes place, the paper and glass should be removed. Seedlings should be pricked out as soon as they can be handled, to give them space to grow.

However, it's no good sowing seeds in January if the temperature is below 60°F. Then a small, electric propagator is a 'must' to get early germination. I have a soil warming cable in a box 5ft by 5ft. The cable is placed in the box, which is first lined with black plastic, then covered with sand or peat which must be kept damp, otherwise the cable will dry out and crack.

In gentle heat sow onions, leeks, summer cabbages (like Golden Acre, Minicole, Hispi and Red Drumhead), cauliflower (All the year Round and Snow Crown), and lettuce (Fortune and All the year Round). I also like to put on a seed dressing, such as Murphy's Combined, for protection against white rot and other fungal diseases.

Vegetable Roly-Poly

A Winter's Warm-You-Up

If bad weather sets in and you have got a bag of flour, some fat and vegetables, this will hold you for the day. Make up suet pastry or dough by mixing:

8oz/225g self-raising flour
¼ teaspoon salt
4oz/100g suet or fat
Cold water to mix

Roll out the suet pastry and sprinkle over with a gravy powder. I use an Oxo and a sprinkling of a few mixed fresh herbs cut up (or dried). Then grate any vegetable which you have by you on to the suet pastry. Salt and pepper to taste. Roll up in a cloth and boil for 3 hours. Serve with a good gravy or some home-made soup.
If you have some rashers of bacon to spare, these cut up and added to the vegetables will improve the flavour of the Roly-Poly.

February

If westerly winds are strong and Candlemas Day (Feb. 2nd) brings cloud and rain, then winter is gone and won't come again.

FEBRUARY is double-faced. The shortest and the worst of all the months, as the French often call it. However, there is always one fine week in February.

As we have only twenty-eight days to endure in February, there is the promise of spring just around the corner. The snowdrop is the flower of the month and is also known as the Candlemas Bell, Mary's Taper and February Fair Maid. But, not only are the flowers starting to wake up, some shrubs are also coming into bloom, like *Viburnum bodnantense.* One of my favourites is *Mahonia* 'Charity' with its long sprays of yellow flowers (they look like lily-of-the-valley); also *Garrya elliptica* is a joy to see with its long, hanging, dark green leaves and extra-long catkins. Then there are the dogwoods, *Cornus alba* and *Cornus mas;* the sweet-smelling *Daphne mezereum* and last of all, witch hazel, *Hamamelis mollis.* We must not forget the winter-flowering heathers, *Erica carnea* and *Erica darleyensis,* providing us with a mass of colour.

At this time of year we have to think about pest and disease control. Spray apples and blackcurrants with Mortegg tar-oil wash to kill over-wintering pests; other fruit buds will be too advanced now for such treatment, as damage could occur. Spray peaches, almonds, nectarines and apricots with a liquid copper fungicide at the very first sign of bud movement, usually about mid-February, to help protect against Peach Leaf Curl. Pick off and burn swollen buds of blackcurrants to remove 'big bud' mites. These pests spread the disease Reversion, which can seriously reduce cropping.

On the subject of pests, the bullfinch can cause a vast amount of damage to fruit buds during the winter. My neighbour has an orchard next to my garden and I see many birds, but the damage done by the bullfinches is unbelievable. For the amateur with a few fruit trees in the garden, I can only suggest that you get a reel of cotton and try and throw it backwards and forwards over the branches of the trees, covering them with the cotton, which may save some of the buds.

A little friend I like to see at this time of year is the hedgehog, Britain's only spring mammal. It's so useful to have around the garden as it feeds on slugs, snails, caterpillars and earthworms. Hedgehogs certainly enjoy a saucer of milk and my father told me that, in his day when a cow lay down, the hedgehog would be accused of taking milk from the udder. I don't think this was true because a cow's udder is tender and it would not like a ball of prickles trying to suck at it! The story should be, I think, that as the cow lies down there would be a leakage from the full udder and the hedgehog would lick up the drips of milk. I have asked some old country boys about this and they agree that a cow would not let a hedgehog suckle it.

After sowing the flowers, it's time to think about trying to sow a few vegetables outside, but this will depend on the weather.

If you can sit on the earth with your trousers down and it feels alright, sow your seeds and they will be up in three days

Parsnip is the first vegetable I like to get in the soil as it takes so long to germinate – about twenty days. I always sow a few radish seeds in the same rows as the parsnips as they come up in seven–ten days, enabling you to see the rows and making it easier for hoeing and keeping clean. My late husband made a marker which marked out three rows at a time, one foot apart, on a good seed bed. He used to reckon that this could be used to mark out drills for any type of seed. The parsnip is a good old stand-by root crop. Years ago it was called the Lent vegetable because it is one root which will stay quite happily in the ground all winter, not being destroyed by frost. I believe (and I think most country people would agree) that a parsnip is no good as a vegetable until it has been well frosted. My late husband used to dig up a few and lay them on top of the soil to get the frost. Good wine can also be made from this excellent root. The varieties which I grow are my old favourite 'Tender and True' and a new F^1 hybrid called 'Gladiator', which grows well in heavy soil, is resistant to canker and has a very good flavour.

A man's sexual powers are believed to be strongly affected by parsley and in some parts of the country parsley wine is an esteemed aphrodisiac. Many people say parsley should be set only by a woman. The ancient Greeks used to sprinkle parsley on the dead; they had a saying that a person who was near to death was in need of parsley, and the roots were much eaten in olden times. I have been told of so many superstitions regarding parsley – one is that you should never take a root from your old home to a new one, as this is supposed to bring bad luck; another is that Good Friday is the day when you should plant the seed as the Devil is powerless, and yet another is that it should not be transplanted, but I have been doing this for years – in fact, I sow first-sowings in February, then prick out into seed trays. If I am going to sow in the garden, I make my drindles (old name for row), then pour a kettle of boiling water in the drindle first, before sowing the seed. This is supposed to help the germination. Don't get worried if you can't see the seed coming up as it sometimes takes five–six weeks to germinate. I would not be without this herb, as it is so useful for cooking and garnishing. I also freeze a lot, it is so simple to do – pick small bunches, wash and pat dry, pop into small bags and straight into the freezer. When taken out to use, it just crumbles up in your hand and it's so useful for soups, stews and stuffing. These are just a few uses, but I could go on and on – I even grow parsley in my flower borders.

Things start to move in February because the days lengthen and the extra light is so important in plant growth. I always say that February is a funny old month; you think you have got over the worst of the winter, then it all starts once more, snow, sharp frosts, winds, the lot. But you can always find a job in the greenhouse. start the gloxinias and begonia corms (in heat), also start to sow some half-hardy annuals like salvias, antirrhinum, lobelia and impatiens (Busy Lizzies). Mustard and cress can be sown every ten

First spring flowers

days or so for salads. Another little tip for green onions is to pot up about six shallots in a 5in container with compost and water, and stand on the windowsill. You will be surprised at how the green shoots come up, so handy for omelettes.

The winter time is when you will appreciate a vegetable garden as you should be enjoying the fruits of your labours. I like to have a saucepan full of good homemade vegetable soup cooking on the stove in cold weather.

Another job I do in February is to pot up my autumn planted geraniums; these are put singly, in 4in pots, but water sparingly as they will rot. Start your trays of dahlias with a little water in early February so that they will send up shoots to use for cuttings.

February is a good time to have a look around the greenhouse for pests, even in winter they are breeding. One particular pest is the Mealy bug; you will find that it is more active in the summer, as the heat seems to draw them out of crevices. The little bugs are pinkish white in colour, covered in a woolly, waxy dust and usually concentrate around the leaf axils. I notice them a lot around my Hoya, so I get a child's paint brush and a small jar of methylated spirit and paint the bugs. The brush helps to kill the eggs of this pest as well. A Malathion insecticide may also be used.

Ox Liver and Parsnip Casserole

1lb/½kg liver
2 rashers bacon (chopped)
1½lb/¾kg parsnips
1oz/25g flour
good pinch salt & pepper
pinch of curry powder
1 cupful of water
1 teaspoon Worcester Sauce
little dripping

Wash and peel the parsnips. Boil for 10 minutes, then slice them thickly. Wash, dry and slice the liver and roll in the flour; season with salt and pepper. Fry the bacon for 5 minutes and put into a hot dish. Fry the liver and parsnips slowly together for 15 minutes keeping them well turned. Put them in the dish with the bacon. Fry the flour brown in the fat from the bacon, stirring it well and then add a little dripping if it is too dry. Pour in the water, sauce and curry, stirring continually until it boils. Boil for 3 minutes and strain over the liver. It is then ready to serve but I like to put mine in a hot oven for 10–15 minutes to allow the gravy to become nice and thick.
Serve with baked potatoes.

March

A peck of March dust is worth a King's ransom

THE PRIMROSE is the plant of the month of March, and what a grand sight it is to see the little yellow faces in the country lanes; they seem to be saying that the cold has gone and warm weather is coming.

In 1881 Queen Victoria sent a wreath of primroses to Benjamin Disraeli and this is when the Primrose League was formed. I used to look forward to picking primroses and violets, making little posies for the children to give to their mothers at the church services on Mother's Day. But over the years they have become scarce, so we leave them to grow on in the green banks and woodlands. On the other hand, look what man has done with the wild primrose.

Over the past twenty years, the seedsmen's meticulous breeding has produced such a mix of colours with every hue you can think of; spotted petals, picotee edged and semi-doubles. Thompson & Morgan of Ipswich have some of the finest strains that I have seen.

Another beautiful sight and sound at this time of the year comes from our feathered friends, the birds. Although I say 'they're hully a nuisance, them spadgers (sparrows), when you find them bathing in the new seed bed, or picking shoots off the peas' I would not miss waking up each morning with my bedroom window open and hearing them in the eaves. Birds sing for many reasons – one is to say that spring is here and another, most important, is to choose a mate. The male (who, by the way, puts on a most wonderful display, showing his plumage to its best advantage) bursts into melody to show his mate what a fine fellow he is. The male is the songster while the female is restricted to calling. Another important reason is for the birds to mark their territory. Robins are particularly nasty to other robins if a pair invade their patch (I have even seen a pair almost kill one poor, little fellow robin). Their song is very alarming if other robins are near and the song will soon change when victory has been achieved. The bird I most like to hear is the blackbird, singing his little heart out whilst sitting on a telegraph pole. It makes one appreciate the free things in life.

A dry March and a showery May portends a wholesome Summer if there be a showery April in between.

So many mists in March, so many frosts in May (I do think that this bit of country lore is true.)

Hopefully, the gardener's year can really begin in March but weather and soil conditions will decide when, and if, seeds can be sown out-of-doors this month.

What a man needs in gardening is a cast iron back with a hinge on it.

If the weather was too damp last month, now is the time to plant your garlic. The bulbs will go a long way as they can be split up; they are called cloves, and you plant them in rows 4in apart. A row of lettuce (All the year Round) and radish can be sown, also a few carrots and peas and one of my stand-bys, a row of perpetual spinach. I know that many people sneer at this vegetable but it is worth its weight in gold when no other vegetable is around – it also freezes very well. Beetroot should be sown at the end of the month. A frame is best used to sow the *Brassica* family, for planting out later on. A few early potatoes may be planted in large pots or tubs in the greenhouse. For June eating, try Suttons Foremost or Maris Bard. At this time of year, a lot of old Brussels sprouts and cabbage stalks will need to be dug out of the garden. A little tip here is not to use your best garden fork for this job, as it will only bend the prongs, or as we say 'spring the sprongs' and the fork will never be the same again. Use an old fork with a couple of broken prongs, as it will do the job just as well. You will often get birds after your 'greens' at this time of year. Try scattering dried powdered garlic around the plants as a deterrent.

March is a good time for planting hedges, evergreen or deciduous. Privet and conifers make for good privacy, as does the beech, which holds its leaves in winter. The holly, too, is worth thinking about although it is slow in growing. Do remember to stake young plants for up to three years. March is also an excellent time to clip back the ivy on walls before the birds start to nest. This is a rather dirty job, but just clip with a pair of shears and brush down with a good stiff broom. The walls may look a bit bare, but new shoots will soon appear. Look out for long shoots which can grow around water troughs and eaves – cut them out or they may do a lot of damage. Look around climbers which are fixed to walls and sheds to see if they need new wall fixings. Also check over-tight ties on trees and climbers, and mend stakes near standard roses.

As soon as snowdrops have faded, lift and divide every three to four years, to increase your stock. Sow sweet peas outdoors where the plants are to flower; I try and soak my seeds in paraffin oil in order to keep the mice away. If you managed to save your pot grown geraniums, abutilons and coleus over the winter, they must be looking rather leggy so this is the time to cut them down to make good cuttings. These will soon root in a sandy compost, then should be placed in a propagator to root further. Don't forget to keep your glass clean so that maximum light reaches the plants. This will be the time when pricking out of delicate seedlings is done and I use an old table fork to ease the seedlings out of the trays. Remember the smaller the seedlings, the quicker they will go ahead for they don't suffer a setback, as larger seedlings may do.

Autumn-fruiting raspberries should be cut down to within 6in of soil level; the canes will be produced in the summer months to fruit in September and October.

Re-pot foliage plants and ferns, also aspidistra. Use a pot one size larger if the plants are over-crowded. Do not feed newly propagated plants as their roots should be encouraged to search for nutrients in the new potting mixture. Ferns like a peat-based mixture. Cacti can also be re-potted using a gritty compost. Hold cacti with a band of folded newspaper when re-potting, as the prickles can be very painful.

Re-seed any lawn patches (this often happens if you have a little

Fragrance of spring

bitch puppy who likes to go outside last thing at night; you will soon see where she 'spends a penny' as the grass will turn yellow and die). If one is planning to sow a new lawn, now is the time to get the plot ready. Apply a general fertiliser over the area, then sow grass seed containing bird deterrent, at about the rate of 1½ oz per square yard.

Lupins and delphiniums can be propagated by cuttings, taking shoots from the root of the plant and then separating a small shoot with a sharp knife. Dip this in rooting powder, potting up with peat and sand and you should have a nice plant.

One golden rule in the garden: Never forget to sow dry and plant wet!

Gladioli should not be planted all at once. It is better to make successive plantings over a period of four to six weeks. Plant the corms on a little bed of sand if on heavy soil (4in deep on 1in of sand). You can also get the dahlias out of winter store and lay them in shallow boxes of peat (I use old grow-bag contents), then water them and you will soon find shoots coming up. Take these for your cuttings when they are 3–4in high, but only do this job if you have a greenhouse. The fuchsia is also a plant that needs to start moving and the first thing to do is pruning. The object of this is to control the size of the plant and ensure that plenty of new wood will result, as the fuchsia only blooms on new wood. This job must be done just before the sap starts to rise. Tap the plant out of the pot, remove as much of the old compost as possible and refill with new compost, using as small a pot as possible. I will tell you more about fuchsias later on.

If the soil is dry and you can rake a good tilth, start to sow cornflowers, larkspur, clarkia and godetia. Mark the patches and rows with sand so that you don't hoe the seed up when weeding the borders. Outdoor early chrysanthemum can be raised from cuttings taken from old stools (roots from plants taken from the garden last autumn). Shoots should be about 2½in long arising from the base of the old plant.

Olive's Spicy Fruit Pie

You are in for a treat with this pie as the pastry has cream cheese mixed with the ingredients. Don't turn your nose up, try it and see!

8oz/225g plain flour
½ teaspoon baking powder
1 level teaspoon salt
4oz/100g butter or margarine
4oz/100g cream cheese or cottage cheese
1 dessertspoon lemon juice
Chilled water

Sift the flour with salt and baking powder. Use fingertips to rub fat in lightly until mixture resembles breadcrumbs. Stir in the cottage or cream cheese, using a knife to mix in cheese as lightly as possible until the mixture is well blended. Mix to a dry dough with the strained lemon juice and a very little chilled water. Knead lightly on a floured board.

Filling: Peel and slice 2 large cooking apples and 2 bananas. Mix 2 tablespoons brown sugar, 1 level teaspoon cinnamon and grated rind of one orange together. Grease a shallow pie dish and fill with alternative layers of fruit and sugar mixture. Pour the juice of the orange over. Moisten edges of the pie and cover with a lid of rolled out pastry. Make hole in centre. Bake in moderate oven 375°F (190°C) or Gas No5 for 20–30 minutes or until pastry is golden brown.

April

April wet, good wheat
April and May are the key to the whole year.
On the third of April comes the cuckoo and the nightingale.

APRIL is the time when we really get down to gardening, I feel. With the increase in daylight and temperature, both plants and pests will be on the move. In the greenhouse young plants will need to be pricked-out into trays. Ventilate well, but remember to close the vents and windows at night as there is still a risk of frost.

Finish the sowing of half-hardy annuals as soon as possible. For a colour display later on, try sowing some coleus, freesias, gloxinias and solanums; and thinking of outside, we should be sowing tender vegetables for planting out later, such as celery, sweet corn, courgettes and tomatoes. You can plant tomatoes in grow-bags, watering the pots well before transferring. I always like to have my grow-bags in the greenhouse a week before needed so that the compost has warmed up. Another tip is to use plastic canes; I put three to each bag and push the canes right through the bag into the soil floor of the greenhouse. This makes sure of firmness and good drainage at the same time. Keep taking cuttings of dahlias, geraniums, fuchsias and Busy Lizzies, using a hormone rooting powder. Onions raised in boxes should be hardened-off. Put these in a garden frame during the next couple of weeks. Do watch for damping-off seedlings, a disease which causes them to collapse where the stem has rotted at the base. Water with Cheshunt compound (a mixture used to check the spread of damping-off disease and other soil-borne fungus diseases, particularly those which attack the stem at soil level). Cheshunt compound is made by mixing two parts by weight of finely-ground copper sulphate with eleven parts by

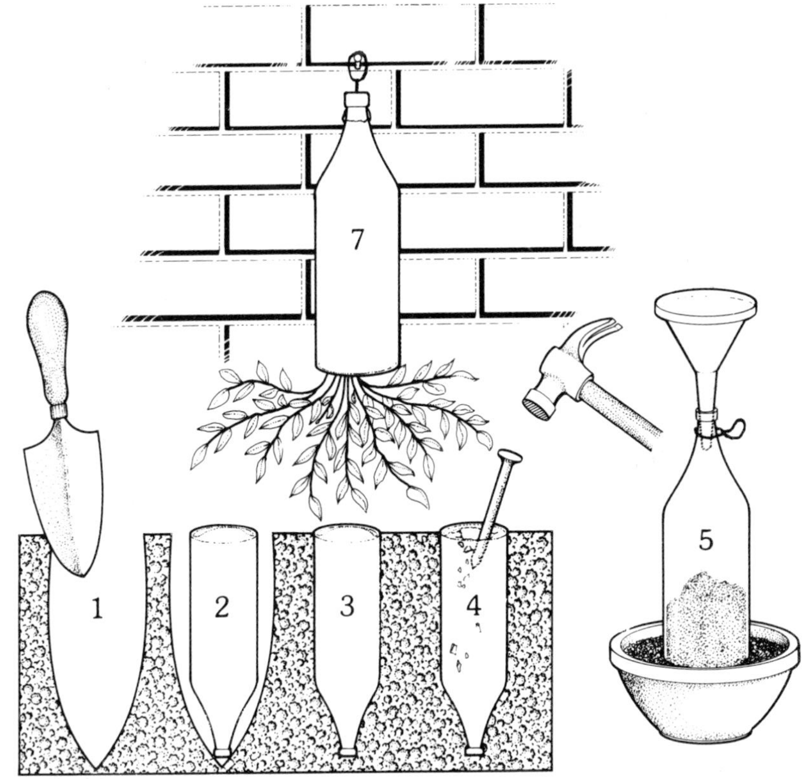

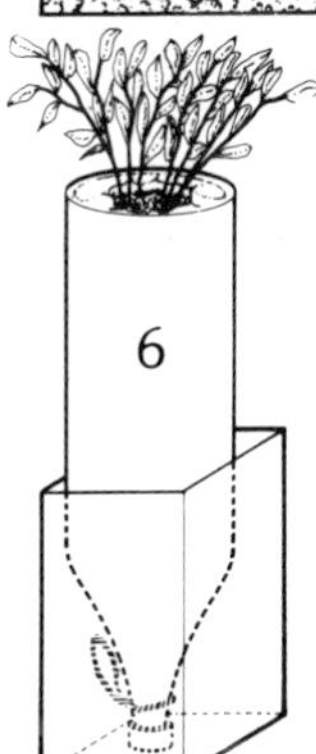

1 Dig hole in soil
2 Insert dimple bottle
3 Pack earth around bottle
4 Tap hole, mid dimple
5 Fill up with compost
6 Keep upside down (after planting cutting), for 6 weeks, use a box
7 Hang bottle on wall or fence, water through neck of bottle

weight of fresh ammonium carbonate. This mixture must be stored in a glass jar with a lid for at least twenty-four hours before use. Afterwards it can be kept for any reasonable length of time. It is prepared for use by dissolving 1oz of the mixture in a little hot water, making up to two gallons with cold water. The solution is sprinkled on the seedlings with the fine rose on the watering-can and should be used as soon as it has been prepared (Don't try to keep some for use later on!)

One is always trying to think ahead when gardening, so if you have still got a bit of room on the greenhouse bench, sow spring flowers for the following year, like foxgloves, forget-me-nots, canterbury bells and polyanthus. The first three mentioned can be sown outside, but I prefer to sow mine in trays and then prick them out. This may seem early to sow but believe me, you do get much better plants. Take the seed heads from daffodils to help to build up the bulbs for next year. Don't tie the leaves down with rubber bands or try to tie them into knots as it won't do the bulbs any good. Be on your guard against narcissus bulbfly. The tiny pest lays its eggs around the neck of the plant in spring when the blooms are fading. Scatter Rootguard or Gamma BHC Dust among your plants especially round the necks. This is also a good time to give the plants a foliar feed to strengthen the growth for next year.

Sweet peas raised under glass early last month can now be planted into their flowering position, when the soil and weather conditions permit. Do try Snoopea and Dwarf Cupid in baskets.

Many people will be thinking about laying a patio, so go in for buying 18in square slabs rather than 24in ones as these are more comfortable to handle. *Think about your poor old back.* They are also not so easily damaged when moving about or storing prior to laying.

When the dog-wood flowers appear,
Frosts will not again be here

If you have a propagation unit, keep the warming cable covered with sand, taking care to keep it damp. If you let it dry out you will soon have trouble with your cable.

Remember to sow more hardy annuals; they will probably germinate more readily now, with the sun giving more power. Those well-spouted potatoes should be planted; the late varieties going in first as they will need a long season of growth, the earlies are early maturing so they can be planted a little later.

The spring flowers will need a little encouragement to burst into flower, such as the auriculas and polyanthus; so give them a little treat like a feed of Liquinure, and include any spring flowers in pots in the greenhouse (cineraria and calceolaria). I prefer to have all my roses pruned by the first or second week in April; cutting hard on my bushes of hybrid tea roses, and moderately on the floribunda or cluster roses, as they are now called. To tackle the job of pruning, just remember to cut out all dead wood and all parts which are damaged or diseased, removing any branch which rubs against another. Remember what I said about pruning an apple tree and throwing your hat through? Well, the same can be said about the rose bushes, they should have an open centre. Do use a good clean pair of secateurs; cut clean, a sloping cut outwards from dormant bud (about 1/4in from bud to cut).

Good hanging baskets are always a joy to see but I think many people go wrong in not planting the baskets soon enough. The sooner they are made up and hung in the greenhouse, the better. Early April is when I start on mine. There are all sorts of baskets and materials to use for lining. Sphagnum moss looks nice if you can get it, but remember to place a shallow dish at the bottom of the basket to act as a water reservoir. They will need little attention apart from daily water, feeding once a week and dead-heading of old blooms and leaves. I put a good pat of cow's dung in the bottom of the basket (on top of the dish), then fill up with a soil-less compost. It will be your choice what you plant as there is such a scope these days for all species of plants – gone are the days of just geraniums and lobelia. Be experimental. I use *Phlox drummondii,* campanulas, petunia, verbena and a popular grey foliage plant of recent years *Helichrysum plicatum,* a pretty plant of slender growth which has silver-grey leaves and yellow flowers in late summer.

My flowering bottles which visitors admire are made up at this time of year. You will need a bottle with a dimple in the bottom –

my brother buries mine in the garden to soil level them taps a hole with a hammer and nail. I then fill the bottles with dry soil-less compost, turn them upside down and plant ivy geranium (or whatever plant you wish) into the hole in the bottle, water, and keep upside down for about six weeks till well rooted. I use old milk crates to stand the bottles in whilst rooting. Put strong twine around the necks of the bottles for hanging on walls. The bottles should be hung in the greenhouse for about six weeks to get the plants established before going outside to decorate the fence and walls.

Spinach Cheese Rissoles

1lb/½kg potatoes
1lb/½kg spinach
2 small eggs
3oz/75g dripping
4oz/100g grated cheese
Breadcrumbs (to fry in)

Boil and mash the potatoes. Cook the spinach making sure that all water is squeezed out. Chop finely, mix with potatoes. Use the beaten egg (keeping a little egg back) to bind all the ingredients, adding salt and pepper. Mould into rissoles and dip into the rest of the egg, then breadcrumbs. Fry in dripping. After you have cooked your rissoles, put grated cheese on top and put under the grill to melt the cheese.

This is a cooked supper dish and a good introduction to those who have never tasted spinach.

May

A misty May and a hot June,
Makes the harvest come right soon

A May flood never did good

I LIKE THE MONTH of May. The garden flowers, such as foxgloves, honesty, pyrethrum and dutch iris are just about to burst out, the blackbird is singing away, and various other birds are nesting about the garden. I often have thrushes and robins nesting in the potting shed, a little wren in the ivy hedge, and behind the shed among the climbing shrubs are house sparrows and blackbirds' nests. I also have two small water ponds in the garden, so in May you can suddenly hear the croak of the frogs and toads (you should always have a toad in the greenhouse, it's lucky). I think the common frog is a lovely creature. The spawning time is very exhausting, for many frogs will die as males fight to win the females. In my part of the country you will see notices saying 'Beware toads and frogs crossing the road', and there are less and less of them around. The frog is the gardener's friend as it eats slugs, snails and earthworms. It catches insects with a rapid flick of the tongue, and a worm is swallowed with the frog scraping the dirt off with its fingers. Slippery food is held in the mouth by minute teeth. I often wonder if man is helping to kill our frogs and toads by putting down all the slug pellets and bait. When I was a small girl I often helped my father, holding the small sack which he brought from the farm after a day's threshing of barley. This was the best way to kill slugs – by putting down a row of barley havels, sharp and prickly. Another remedy was old soot which used to stand at the top of the garden for up to a year, then was put in rows around the vegetable and flower beds.

May is the month of Maia, the White Goddess. White blossom is white hawthorn and she presides over the spring growth. I feel that May can be a tricky month, as often you can get sharp frosts.

A swarm of bees in May,
Is worth a load of hay

Now back to gardening jobs. It is time to do some thinning out of vegetables such as parsnips, 6–9in apart and carrots, about 1in apart. It is advisable to choose a dull day or evening for this task. I like to put a little Jeyes Fluid on carrots after this job has been done, (1 teaspoon to 2 gallons water). Beetroot should be about 2½–3in apart – I leave mine rather close, then I take beet out about as big as a 10p piece and pickle them in vinegar (very nice for Christmas presents).

The weather should now be getting warmer and the sun more powerful, so try and do some shading in the greenhouse. Use powder like Summer Cloud, and mix up in a bowl. I put mine on with a soft broom, but be careful not to break your glass by being too heavy-handed. Stand cans of water in the greenhouse to take the chill off and start to harden off bedding plants. Canes can be put up for runner beans, and early potatoes lightly earthed-up; if they are too big to cover, try covering the tops with straw or even newspapers, but this is only if a frost warning has been forecast. Sweetcorn can be planted out now but will do better planted in groups rather than straight lines across the vegetable plot, as this gives greater chance of pollination. Marrows and cucumbers can be planted out in the second–third week in May. Now is the time to prune early spring-flowering shrubs, like flowering currant and forsythia, and take the tops out of broad beans, watching out for blackspot. I remember mother used to save washing-up water for Dad to use on the broad beans for blackfly. Mother never had any washing-up liquid in those days, all she used was common soda in the water. Strawberries should be strawed when the fruit has formed. If you have a small patch, carefully put the stems with strawberries on in a jam jar (to keep away from the blackbirds).

One has always to think about next year, so this is the time for sowing wallflowers, sweet william, honesty, canterbury bells and forget-me-nots (the end of May will do for these sowings). Stake the herbaceous border. Use twiggy sticks if you can get hold of some (even these are a job to find these days), they look more natural. Delphiniums are better supported by a cane.

When outdoor bulbs have finished, remove the old flower heads to avoid setting seed, which will exhaust the bulb. Give them a general fertiliser to encourage the making of a large bulb for next year's flowers. Also don't forget to leave the foliage until it has died down and turned brown. Some people like to tie a knot in the leaves, as I mentioned with daffodils, but this does not help to build the bulb up and often disease sets in the foliage and runs down into the bulb. Remember that a well-kept lawn sets off the rest of the garden to the greatest advantage, but regular attention is needed to keep the grass looking at its best; keeping it green, healthy and free of weeds all through the season. I am proud of my grass as my brother keeps it trim and gives it a feed every two weeks throughout the summer. Ron swears by keeping it trim and sometimes cuts mine three times a week by using a hand push mower.

Evergreens can be cut back at the end of May. Privet, Lawson *Cupressus, Thuya plicata* and *Cupressocyparis leylandii* are all best if well trimmed in late May.

Hanging baskets can also be put out in May, but remember that they are outside and don't leave them just for the rain to water them! I think the most important points are never allow them to dry out and feed them regularly. I take mine down once a week and immerse them in an old bath, making sure that they are soaked. Once a basket dries out, it will never look the same. Regularly remove old flower heads and don't be afraid to replace the odd plant that is past its best.

Don't forget that May is the highlight of the gardener's calendar and if you wish to see gardens and flowers at their superb best visit the Chelsea Flower Show. This is one trip that I never like to miss – you can always see a new flower or shrub which you would like in your garden.

However, May can be a dangerous month in that it may be sunny and quite dry but 'hold hard'; be on your guard for sharp frosts. I have known serious frost on the 15th and 16th May. On the other hand, we can experience some of the hottest days of the year – so often when you need to put out bedding plants, the land is dry as a bone. This is where mulching comes in and one of the best products on the market is 'Cambark'. This is a wood bark cut into small pieces and not only does it conserve moisture, it stops the weeds and rubbish from growing and forms an attractive background for all your plants. Herbaceous perennials will now be growing very tall in the borders, so thin out the weak shoots to get better flowers, and stake and tie-in the plants – twiggy branches from apple tree prunings come in handy for use in the flower borders. In fact, all tree prunings can be put to some use in the garden.

Gooseberry in a Hurry Pudding

As the first gooseberries come into season, this is a simply made-up sweet for the unexpected dinner guests.

1¼lb/600g gooseberries
3oz/75g sugar
Brown bread
1–2oz/50g butter
2oz/50g mixed peel (or grated rind of lemon)

First top and tail gooseberries. Cook until nearly soft, add peel and sugar. Line a dish out with sliced bread. Pour over the juice from the gooseberries. Tip some of the fruit into the dish, then another layer of bread. Add remaining gooseberries. Finish up with layer of bread, adding a few knobs of butter on top, plus a shaking of brown sugar to make top crisp. Bake in hot oven for 15 minutes.

(My mother used to make this pudding using apples and, if she hadn't enough bread, cornflakes instead.)

⋙ June ⋘

A dripping June sets all in tune

A swarm of Bees in June is worth a silver spoon

A leak in June brings Harvest soon

I ALWAYS THINK THAT JUNE is a rewarding month in the garden. Hardy, herbaceous perennials and flowering shrubs give masses of colour, and the roses are coming into their first bloom. We always have our church fete at this time of the year in the vicarage, and the walls of the vicarage are covered with roses, like 'New Dawn' and 'Albertine'. I also have a couple of favourties in my garden – the shrub rose 'Rose Mundi' whose small pale pink flowers are distinctly striped with crimson on twiggy upright bushes, and 'Roseraie-de-l'Hay', a much bigger shrub rose. This is one of the best of Rugosas; the only fault I find is that it does not have hips like other Rugosas, but its petals are super for making rose petal wine.

This month can also bring high temperatures, and one of the miseries is hay fever. Gardeners who suffer from hay fever must be the unluckiest group of people. Can you think of anything more frustrating than having to run for cover to a darkened room to get over a miserable attack of itchy eyes and runny nose when you are enjoying working in your garden? Some relief is gained by taking drugs, but a simple remedy is to wear dark glasses for a few hours a day. The main hay fever triggers in Britain are the silver birch, elm and alder, and also ryegrass; so remember to wear sunglasses when near such trees and plants

But back to the vegetable patch. This is a busy time when plants will quickly grow. Make sure that repeat sowings of salad crops are made for continuity of supply. Plants like winter cabbage, cauliflower, Brussels sprouts and broccoli should be ready to lift from their seed beds and be planted out. Lift carefully, making sure to water first and plant firmly, watering in after planting. Towards the end of June leave cutting asparagus as this will give it time to build up good root for the following year. You can plant outside tomatoes, marrows and leeks (I like to put my leeks in where first spring cabbages have grown, after a good few wheelbarrow loads of muck have been dug in). Take the tops out of broad beans, cook and serve with cheese.

Tomatoes in the greenhouse will need a weekly application of a high potash feed to ensure good cropping; daily attention will also be required to watering and ventilation. Watch out for whitefly – it doesn't take long for an infestation to build up. I like to use smoke cones, but you must repeat this treatment in a week. Potato blight can be expected if we get warm and damp weather so spray with liquid copper fungicide. Another little pest about this time is the flea beetle which eats small holes in foliage. Put derris dust on the rows. I also like to thin out my carrots again, then I go down the rows with a weak solution of Jeyes Fluid.

Now to the flower garden. Do keep plenty of water bowls around the garden for the birds. Even old hub-caps from cars will do, and you will be surprised how many birds like to keep one container to themselves. It's lovely to see house martins and swallows arriving and darting to the ornamental pools for water and if you are lucky you may actually see a dragonfly. They are among the fastest flying and most colourful of insects. Their speed varies from 35mph to 60mph – I told you that you would have to be quick to spot them!

Hanging baskets should be put outside now if you decided against putting them out in May. Avoid a draughty position and choose a site where the baskets can be watered easily.

Many early-flowering shrubs such as forsythia, deutzia and philadelphus should be pruned this month by removing the old flowering wood, but do use sharp secateurs.

Look out for the roseleaf sawfly, it can be bad in June. The leaves of the shrubs curl up lengthwise and often the caterpillar has gone by the time you see the trouble. You can help by removing and burning some of the leaves and try spraying with Malathion on a warm, still evening.

It should be safe to bed out all border plants. Do try a bed of impatiens, they make good bedding plants and will also thrive in shade. I grow very attractive baskets of the varieties called 'Blitz' and 'Futura' and all F[1] hybrids. Spring bulbs may now be lifted, but if they are still green dig a trench and lay a piece of wire netting in the bottom of the trench. Put the bulbs in and cover with soil leaving the ends of the wire netting sticking out. When the bulbs are dry just lift the wire netting up, bulbs and all. This little tip helps you to keep the bulbs all in one compact area. Dahlias will now require tying up to stakes or canes, as one rough wind may easily destroy the plants. This treatment also goes for tall border plants such as delphiniums and lupins.

June is a good time to preserve herbs. They should be picked just before they flower. I like to freeze mine because I find that they retain the natural flavour. Just cut and wash in boiling water for a few seconds to set the colour, pat them dry, put into small plastic bags and deep freeze. Alternatively, you can chop up the herbs and fill ice-cube trays, top up with water and freeze. Put the frozen cubes in a plastic bag for storage – these come in handy when making soups.

If the Cuckoo sings after St. John's day, June 24th,
the Harvest will be late

Cut your thistles before St. John's
You will have two instead of one

We are now at the stage when the lawn will need irrigating and feeding. Spike the compacted areas. My brother always says that a lawn sets off the garden, especially with cut edges plus a good feed with 'Green up' (Synchemicals). Another precautionary tip – we often get sudden and severe winds in June, so give extra protection to plants like runner beans as wind will do more harm to them than one can imagine. This is often the time when newly-planted trees and shrubs which were set-in last autumn or spring will suffer if we get wind and hot weather. Wind can rock them about, leaving a hole around the bottom of the stem, so fill in the hole and stamp well round the tree. Give it a good watering (not just a couple of pints) then give a good mulch so that the moisture will not evaporate. Cover your strawberries. Also put down slug bait or pellets. Give a spray against mildew, like Benlate.

Try to sow salad vegetables every two weeks to see you through the summer. But remember when sowing radish that they do need a lot of water. If the weather is hot and dry sow 'Little Gem' lettuce or 'Cos' lettuce. I find that they do not go to seed like other varieties. Remember to put your shading on the greenhouse as the sun strengthens, or your plants can soon be scorched up. Watch out for the carrot fly and cabbage root fly. I like to go down the rows with Jeyes Fluid (2 teaspoons to 2 gallons water). I always do this, or my brother does, after we have thinned out the carrots. Pick a dull day to do this job, when the sun won't lay the plants down to ground level.

Nasturtium Sauce

2 pint jug pressed down with nasturtium flowers
2 pints/1150ml vinegar
6 shallots, cut up
8 cloves
1 teaspoon salt
1 teaspoon cayenne pepper
1 tablespoon brown sugar
½oz/13g turmeric
1 tablespoon Indian soy

Mix the turmeric with a little of the vinegar, then add all the other ingredients (except the flowers and Indian soy). Simmer for 10–15 minutes. Pour over the flowers while hot. Cover closely and stand for 1 week. Strain and pour into bottles before corking. Add Indian soy. This is a nice sauce to have with cold meats.

»»»» July ««««

St. Swithins Day if thou dost rain,
For forty days it will remain.
St. Swithins Day if thou be fair,
For forty days twill rain nae mair

IN SOME COUNTRIES it was believed that if rain fell on St Swithins Day (15th July) and christened the apples, it was a good-luck omen. This month is the gourmet's delight, with all the fruits and vegetables coming into the kitchen from the garden. There is nothing better than the first new potatoes and fresh green peas, succulent carrots, courgettes and beetroots; also the strawberries, raspberries and blackcurrants. It's the time when my freezer starts to fill up, as I often put early fruit in the freezer and make my jams and wine at a later date. This is also a good time of the year to use rose petals for a number of kitchen purposes, like making your own rose water, so useful in sponges and ice cream as well as a good hand-lotion. Rose water was known as early as 140 BC. The deep scented red roses are the best because they have a strong perfume and colour the water pale pink. Fill a pan with red rose petals (remove any white heel as this has a bitter flavour), cover the petals with water and keep at boiling point but do not boil. After an hour, remove petals and add fresh ones. Repeat until the desired strength has been reached. Strain and bottle.

Rose vinegar is a joy to have in the store cupboard and it's so simple to make. I use a large coffee jar, half-filled with rose petals and covered with white vinegar. This is left to steep for two days on the window sill in the sun, then strained. You will find this is useful for putting on a fruit salad. The French ladies used rose vinegar for headaches by shaking a little of the vinegar on a handkerchief, for its cooling and refreshing effect. My dear mother used plain vinegar on a white handkerchief and tied it around her head; or if she had run out of vinegar, a common dock leaf or even strips of cucumber were used, placed on the forehead. We can find so many uses for our garden produce; not just for vegetables but flowers and weeds as well.

But back to the garden. Potato blight can be a problem with moist weather this month. You will notice dark brown patches around the edges of the leaves, which spread rapidly. Spray Bordeaux Mixture. This disease can be worse in tomatoes, as the spores blow from the potato crop. You will first see when the disease is present by the large, brown, marbled areas on the green fruit, plus dark brown streaks on stems and leaves.

If you wish to have plenty of colour in the garden, dead flower heading should be regularly carried out. Removing the dead heads not only keeps the garden looking tidy but also encourages your plants to keep on flowering. This is also the time to start feeding your plants. My brother starts weekly feeding with Phostrogen. This is the in-between time, as all the bedding has been set out, the vegetable garden is all planted and providing fresh crops, and there is plenty of fresh fruit coming up.

Do remember to prune fruit bushes after fruiting, especially regular pruning for blackcurrants, cutting out all the old wood to make way for younger growth. With red and white currants cut back each of the shoots forming the head of a good bud about 4in from the base, which will encourage the formation of new shoots. Red and white currants are much slower in growth than blackcurrants. Gooseberries require little pruning, only the removal of dead wood, or if there is overcrowding in the centre of the bush. Thinking about fruit, we have the problem of wasps at this time of the year. If you do get stung, take an onion, cut it in half and rub on the sting; this makes an excellent remedy. My dad used to get a jam-jar which had a little jam left in the bottom and fill it quarter-full with water – you'd be surprised to see how many wasps were killed in this way. You would always see a jar hanging near the back door of cottages years ago containing jam and water – or perhaps wine!

Summer glory

Tomatoes under glass, will be growing fine by now, but remember to take side shoots out. The best time to do this is in the morning, as they snap-off better at this time rather than in the evenings. Another tip I was given by an old gardener was to start feeding your tomatoes when the first truss was set, giving a weekly feed. When second truss is set, feed twice a week and the third truss, feed three times weekly. We can start to harvest some of our garden produce this month. The old custom with shallots was to plant on the shortest day and harvest on the longest, but I find that this depends on your soil. If it's wet and heavy you have to leave it till it's fit to stand on. When lifting shallots, be careful. Don't yank them straight out of the ground, just get a fork and prise them gently out of the soil, leave for two or three days then break up each cluster and spread out in the sun on an old piece of wire netting to dry and harvest. Do let the air circle around them, and then store in a dry place. You will know when the shallots are ready to harvest as the tops, or leaves, will start to wither.

This is the month to start preserving your herbs. Here is a good tip I was given for storing mint: get a jar three-quarters filled with golden syrup and put into this as much mint (chopped) as possible, then store in the refrigerator. When you need mint sauce, take a little of the mixture from the jar and dilute with a little vinegar. This will last well into the winter months.

Celery and celeriac need plenty of water whilst growing; also slugs love celery so I put slug pellets in the celery trench, plus a little salt – my father always used barley chaff, but you can't get this nowadays. Marrows and courgettes will need plenty of water too, and feeding every seven days. Cyclamen corms which have been laying in pots on their sides can be restarted into growth. Just scratch away the top inch of soil, re-pot with fresh compost and give the pot a good soaking. Stand your pot in shade and increase the water as the plant grows. The plant will appreciate a spray if you have the time, mornings and evenings. Remember to take cuttings from fuchias, geraniums and other house plants. Ivies do very well at this time of the year – they come in so useful for coffee mornings and charity sales. Plants always sell well.

All winter greens should be planted by the middle of July. Spray the ground first with Jeyes Fluid. Last of all, keep the hoe going. Regular hoeing lets the air into the land and plants will grow much better as a result.

Some old sayings:
Hoe before rubbish comes, not when the land is covered with weeds.

It is an ill labourer that quarrels with his tools.
Neither wise nor fools can work without tools.
Only fools will lend their tools.
What is a workman without his tools.

Blackcurrant and Almond Paste Tart

This is unusual, but very good

1 egg
6oz/150g castor sugar
1 lemon
½lb/225g ground almonds
6oz/150g icing sugar
Few drops vanilla essence
1lb/½kg blackcurrants
Arrowroot } cook together
Sugar }

Make a deep flan case with almond paste and fill this with blackcurrants which have been stewed in sugar and water. Bind the syrup with a little arrowroot. Eat this flan cold, with shortbread fingers or sponge fingers. *To make the almond paste:* Sieve the castor sugar with an equal quantity of icing sugar and mix in a basin with ground almonds and a dessertspoonful of lemon juice. Flavour with a few drops of vanilla essence. Knead the mixture well with the hand until it is smooth, adding beaten egg to moisten as you want it. You can then roll out and fit the flan dish.

August

Dry August and warm,
Does harvest no harm,
A rainy August makes a hard bread crust

AUGUST is often the holiday month for many people and we sometimes have cuttings from friends to try in our gardens. Shrubs will take quite easily if you dig a trench in a shady part of your garden. Put in some peat and sharp sand, then the cuttings, like buddleia, hypericum, pyracantha, hydrangea and many more. Firm soil down well, water and leave until the following year. Take geranium cuttings too – I cut mine from the plant and leave for two–three hours to dry off, then put four or five cuttings in a 5in pot and stand outside away from direct sunshine.

It's time to sow spring cabbages for next year, but the variety called Spring Hero should be sown two weeks later. My 'everlasting' flowers are coming into colour now, so they need to be picked, put into small bunches and hung up in the shed to dry. Do pick as soon as you see a little colour – if you leave them until they are fully out, the middle of the flower heads will drop out. Helichrysums in particular will do this!

Climbing and rambling roses will be ready for tying-up and old flowering growths removed. After pruning, train long shoots to frames or fences. Perennials will be looking their best but I think August is a good time to assess the garden and make plans for any alterations you want to make, like moving plants too short for the back of the border to the front and vice-versa. It is also a good time to think about laying new lawns. Do prepare the soil well, dig over, rake down and pick off all stones and debris. Try to get a good tilth, it pays if you rake soil several times. Firm the soil evenly so that there is no risk of settlement.

Rhubarb leaves will have died down so this is the time to lift and divide the crowns, leaving a few spare crowns on the surface to be frosted. They can then be potted or boxed up later for forcing.

This is the time of year when flower shows are in full swing and it is handy to carry a note pad and pencil to these events so one can write down the names of varieties of vegetables and flowers. Every year more colourful and bigger flowers appear and it reminds me of one of the verses on a stone plaque in my garden:-

The Gardener's Prayer

O Lord, please listen to my prayer,
As I sit here upon my chair,
I've cut the hedge and mowed the lawn,
And planted seeds from early morn,
And now I pray you make them grow,
Like the pictures on the packets show.

Visitors and holidaymakers like to visit gardens and one remark we are always hearing is that we pack so much in a small space! How and why? We use a lot of containers as well as bedding-out annuals so that we can get different heights. I do love to see the wheelbarrows and old chimney pots planted with *Abuliton thompsonii,* it's large maple-like leaves, heavily mottled with yellow, intermingled with plants of *Verbena venosa,* clusters of mauve flowers – also troughs of *Calceolaria* 'Rugosa Midas' and *Mimulus* 'Calypso'. But they will need feeding every week, plus watering sometimes twice a day. Sweet peas will also be at their best (if you suddenly see the buds drop, it is often from lack of water) and plenty of feeding is necessary because vigorous growth is being made. Try and give moist soil a good mulching with peat or composted bark.

Pot up some freesias and *Nerine bowdenii* from mid-August. Take freesia corms and plant them 2–3in apart in pots. Don't overwater, in fact they do best being on the dry side. Stand pots in a cool place in full light for a period of six weeks. Nerines should be started into growth in a cool greenhouse. The necks should show above compost level.

Glorious harvest festival

Gladiolus can be lifted and dried-off. Save some of the small corms as they can be sown next spring. It takes about three years to get flowers from small bulblets. Stop outside grown tomatoes by pinching out the tops, but keep feeding them till the end of the month. Sweet corn should be ready to harvest – to test if fit, the cob should exude a creamy liquid if pressed with the thumb. Runner and French beans will need to be picked daily, so if you go on holiday do arrange for them to be picked or they will grow coarse and old, or even stop growing altogether. I still think that the best way to preserve green beans is cut up and packed in large sweet jars. Put in one layer of beans, then a layer of block salt. To use, take out some beans, soak well then boil in the usual way, drain and serve with butter.

New strawberry beds can be made with runners which were pegged down in July; they should have made good roots by now and can be cut from the parent plants. Also at this time it is best to sow a row of winter spinach, as this will help out with the green vegetables during the winter months. Main crop potatoes can be taken up at the end of August, making sure that the skins are set. If left in heavy soil, the slugs will start to eat them! Also Japanese onions can be sown, for harvesting next June, and you can put two or three rows of leeks out now – no need to dig the ground, just rake and level. Make holes 8–10in deep and 12in apart. I like to cut the top foliage off to about 2in (they only flag, then the birds pull them up). Just drop the leek in the hole, don't fill in the hole, and water thoroughly to settle the roots.

August is also the time to collect flower seeds, but use paper bags for collections as plastic makes the seeds sweat. There is no point in saving F^1 or hybrid seeds as they will not be 'true' next time. Make sure that dahlias and chrysanthemums are staked and tied, and put some flower pots on the stakes, upside down, to catch the earwigs. The pots must be emptied daily and earwigs destroyed.

Looking ahead to Christmas, now is the time to pot up some early paper white narcissus and hyacinths for the festival season – but do buy prepared bulbs for potting up.

Stuffed Vegetable Marrow

1 small marrow
½lb/225g cooked meat (minced beef, ham or boiled bacon etc)
1 small chopped onion
Few sprigs of parsley chopped up
2–3oz/75g bread crumbs
1 egg
¼lb/100g chopped mushrooms
Salt and pepper
1 teaspoon Worcester sauce
Oxo or Bovril
Few oat flakes

Cut marrow into two and then in halves lengthwise, peel and remove seeds and steam until almost soft. This is where a lot of people go wrong with their stuffed marrow; you must almost cook the marrow before stuffing is added. You then put chopped onion and mushrooms in a frying pan with a little dripping, cook about 10 minutes until soft. Add rest of ingredients, turn into a bowl and mix well with beaten egg. Season well. You will then need to add some Oxo or Bovril. Better still, if you have some spare stock in the fridge, use this, about ½ pint. Stuff marrow sections. Sprinkle with few oat flakes and a dot of margarine. Put in greased dish and bake in hot oven for 15 minutes. This is good served with baked potatoes.

September

September blow soft,
Till the fruits are in the loft

EVERYONE LIVING in the country thinks of harvest, so the following words come to mind: 'All is safely gathered in, Ere the winter storms begin'. Out of the earth came full breath.

Many gardens have small pools or water gardens where trees are planted nearby. Now is the time to make a frame of one inch wire netting to cover the pool, to keep decaying leaves from falling in. I lost all my fish one year as they were unable to get any oxygen.

As the nights get colder watch the ventilation in the greenhouse. Clear out old tomato and cucumber plants which have finished growing. 'Cleanliness is next to godliness.' It's time to give the greenhouse a good clean. Wash all the structure work with Jeyes Fluid. Winter light is so important under glass so I clean my glass with bleach and washing up liquid. Red spider mite should be dealt with before it goes into hibernation. Burn a sulphur candle but be sure to empty the greenhouse first. Ease up on the watering; try to water early mornings, as too much water later in the day will start off botrytis (a grey, fluffy mould often seen in geranium leaves). Talking of geraniums – try sowing some seeds this month to get nice plants before winter. Geranium seeds need a miniumum soil temperature of 70° to 75°F and temperature fluctuation can cause delay in germination. I find that you get early flowers if sown at this time of year. As I write, I look out of my window and see a hanging-basket of 'Summer Showers' – trailing ivy leaf geraniums. So many visitors admire them as they have been in bloom all summer (from seed to flower in seventeen weeks).

When gloxinias, begonias and achimenes (hot water plants)

finish flowering, turn the pots on their sides on the greenhouse bench to dry-off. *Erythronium* (dog's-tooth violet) may now be planted. The tuberous roots like rich soil; this is a lovely flower coming into bloom late April and May. Another favourite flower of mine is the lily. 'Consider the lilies of the field, they toil not neither do they spin. And yet I say unto you that even Solomon in all his glory was not arrayed like one of these.' The lily was admired and held sacred long before the start of the Christian era. To the Greeks, it was a symbol of purity, and this association with purity was confirmed when the lily became the flower of the Virgin Mary. This is the Madonna Lily; pure white and wonderfully perfumed it has been cultivated for over 3,000 years. So many people think that this superb plant is difficult to grow, but this is untrue. You can get lilies in every colour, but some lilies have dislikes in certain soil conditions; as a generalisation, most like free-draining soil rich in humus. Don't forget that they like their heads in the sun and their roots in the shade (just like the clematis). Varieties grow from one to ten feet tall, so check the height if you are planning to make a border. I grow a lot in pots as they make nice patio plants. Good varieties for this purpose are *Enchantments lilium* and *Lilium specoisum.* I leave them in pots for three years, then plant out in the garden and start again.

Lawns will still need cutting, but raise the height of the blade 1/4in above the summer cutting height. Lawn repairs may now be carried out.

If you have a passion flower, cut out the shoots to prevent over-crowding as soon as the flowers fade, but do watch that you don't cut out all the lateral shoots or you will not get any flowers next year. We often get gloriously sunny days in September, but insects can be pests at this time of the year. To prevent insect bites, put some bruised elder leaves in your old garden hat – this will keep them away. Don't forget to plant a few flower seeds to stand the winter and hopefully you should get some early blooms next

Some welcoming colours in the greenhouse for visitors to see; ivies, geraniums and *nepeta (Clive Howard)*

A quiet corner of my garden – among rosa mundi, alliums and conifers *(Clive Howard)*

spring. Cornflower, shirley poppies, nigella (Love-in-a-mist), larkspur, candytufts (Iberis), and dwarf mixed are a few popular varieties. My father always had a border of candytuft round our cottage garden. When it comes to clearing the garden, think about the blind or people with poor eyesight if you are pulling up nice scented plants. Pot up one or two like 'Lady Plymouth, Little Gem', or the oak leaf varieties of geraniums, which all smell nice; even a few cuttings of lavendar. We seem to throw so much away in the autumn when someone else would appreciate a plant.

Harvesting the first of the apples and pears takes place now. People often ask how we know when the fruit is fit for picking from the tree. To check this, put your hand under the fruit, lift it and give a gentle twist. If it is ready, the fruit will part easily from the tree. Don't be in a hurry to gather the fruit before it is ready. Now is also a good time to look for puff balls (mushroom family) if you have an orchard; or sometimes they grow beside the country lanes. They are good eaten when young, sliced and fried with some bacon.

Now is the time to think again about next year, so plant out spring cabbage, hyacinth allium and other spring bulbs as the summer bedding plants are cleared away. Harvest any remaining potatoes which are still in the ground and take the precaution of drying the tubers for a few hours in the sun after lifting. In my younger days the small potatoes which we called 'chats' were kept separate and boiled up for the chickens' food in winter.

Those of you who planted out the solanum (Christmas cherry) in late spring, should now lift them and pot up for the winter. Delphinium, eryngium, gaillardia and many other herbaceous plants can be split up. I pot a lot of pieces and stand them in the garden frame; they come in useful for sales at coffee mornings etc next spring.

Wishing you well – with various annuals! *(Author)*

Somewhere in there is the back door, hidden by begonias, fuchsias and *impatiens (Author)*

The fruits of labour

Gooseberries and currants may now be propagated, so ask a friend for a few cuttings from his or her bushes. If you would like trees and shrubs which produce coloured berries try *Berberis thunbergii*, *Pyracantha atalantioides*, symphoricarpos (snowberry) and of course, many more.

Bullace Wine

(An old-fashioned yellow plum which used to grow around cottage gardens years ago)

6–6lb/2–3kg bullaces
2½–3lb/1½kg sugar
8oz/225g raisins
1 gallon/4½ l water
1oz/25g wine yeast
1oz/25g yeast nutrient
1 tablespoon pectic enzyme
(this helps to break down the fruit)

Wash fruit and put into a fermenting bucket. Pour over boiling water. When cool, add the pectic enzyme. Stir well and cover. Leave 24 hours before adding yeast nutrient. Cover and leave 3 days stirring daily. Strain onto sugar, cover for another 2 days, keeping warm. Pour into a fermenting jar and ferment. Leave 9 months to 1 year before drinking. (I think that all fruit wines should be kept at least one year before drinking.)

October

Fresh October brings the Pheasant,
Then to gather nuts is pleasant

OCTOBER IS ONE of my favourite times in the garden. The weather is often warm and pleasant, and you also have the fruits of the garden coming in for pickling, jam making and wine. It is also harvest festival time and I love to see all the produce arranged around the church – windows filled with chrysanthemums and dahlias intermingled with carrots, onions, potatoes, apples and beetroot. Then there is the large marrow with the name of the church scratched on it (this is done when the marrow is young – if you scratch the name on the skin of the marrow, with any sharp tool, you will be surprised how the letters grow as the marrow also keeps growing). Autumn leaf colours can be so rich, even if it is only for a short time. Berries also are pretty with golds, reds and orange, but do watch children if you are out with them for a walk. The berries of the deadly nightshade (Solanum) are very poisonous, and these red and black berries are often seen on hedgerows at this time of year.

Pull up old tomatoes that were grown outside. I pull off all the tomatoes and stand in a 2½ dozen egg tray, standing in a box and covered; but first make sure to put a red tomato on each tray. This will give off a gas, ethyl, which will ripen the green ones.

If you did not get round to washing the greenhouse last month, do it soonest. Make sure that all shading is removed from the glass. I also like to get my bubble polythene up before the end of October as it does help to keep the cost of heating bills down. You should be ready to bring in all pot plants that have been standing in the garden – geraniums, fuchsias etc. Do check underneath the pots for slugs and give them a spray with a fungicide.

(Also check the heathers.) Keep an eye too on the celery. Dark-brown spots indicate an attack of leaf spot. Spray with liquid copper fungicide. Finish getting the spring cabbage planted and the rest of the potatoes out. Do store in paper sacks (or old hessian sacks if you can still get hold of them!) Plastic bags will only make them sweat and go rotten.

It is time to think about storing vegetables, so out come my old tin baths and I fill these up with carrots and beetroot, using the dry contents of the old grow-bags in which I grew my tomatoes. Start with a layer of compost in the bottom of the bath, then a layer of vegetables, working neatly in rings till you end up with a layer of compost on top. You can use dry sand instead of old compost. Just one thing; do wring the tops of beetroot since if you cut the tops off they will bleed and will lose their colour.

Once the old plants are cleared you can think about compost on the land. Order a good load of farmyard muck if you can get it! Cows muck is best, well rotted (I once lost cucumbers and peppers in the greenhouse by using fresh pig manure; there was too much ammonia and the gas killed the plants). Remember well rotted is the answer with all manure.

In October dung your field,
And your land its wealth will yield

As the hanging baskets have finished for the summer, make up a basket for the winter. Try planting small ivy ferns and a grey plant of *Cineraria senecio,* 'Silver Dust'; it makes a nice contrast with greens and greys. You can also use pansies and polyanthus for a bit of colour. Another idea is to plant a basket with parsley and hang up out of the frost. You can have it in the kitchen so long as it doesn't get too warm – try the variety 'Afro' which has tightly curled leaves.

Christmas will be the next subject to occupy your thoughts. If you go for country walks, don't forget to pick the sloes, for sloe wine or sloe gin. Then there are the blackberries. I know there is an old saying that you should not pick blackberries after Michaelmas day, as the Devil spits on them, but I have found the nicest ones in the middle of October. Crab apples, wild damsom, hawthorn, hips and elderberries all make good wine and jellies.

In the garden, save your poppy heads (you can paint them all colours later on). Then you have honesty (silver pennies) and pampas grass. This should be picked when the feathers are just green, and only just coming out. If you have forgotten to pick it and it is now fully out, spray with hair lacquer to hold the fluffy feathers. Clear the borders of summer plants and fork in some compost or top-dress with Growmore fertiliser. You are then ready to plant pansies, violas, myosotis (forget-me-not) and polyanthus. You will probably have to put black thread over the top of the last mentioned flowers as the birds love to pick the bright colours out of the centre of the plant. Wallflowers and cheiranthus make a nice show but if you purchase plants do beware as these can bring club-root into your garden (they are a member of the brassica family). Herbaceous borders can be tidied up. Cut down all flowering material to about 4in high. Fork over and split up any large clumps, remembering to use the outside new growth of these clumps and discard the old centres.

I am reminded of the saying of country folk when leaves are falling; 'Plant trees at All Hallowtide and you're sure they will prosper. Plant them after Candlemas and you'll have to beg them to grow'. (All Hallowtide is October 21st and Candlemas Day is February 2nd.) So now you know the best time for planting trees and shrubs.

As the colder days approach we have to think about lifting tender roots like *Lobelia cardinalis* and blue salvias (*patens*). I take several cuttings from tender plants like gazanias, osteopernum (Star of the Veldt) and pestemons.

Reduce watering the pot plants but continue to feed those plants which are still in growth such as the fuchsia and pelargonium families. Cyclamen, cineraria and primula will need feeding every ten days or so.

Have you ever thought of having fresh herbs for winter use? Box up a few roots of mint and roots of parsley, as these can be grown in a cool greenhouse.

Pickled Brussels Sprouts

2lb small tight, very fresh sprouts
2 pints/1200ml white malt vinegar
1 tablespoon mixed pickling spices
2oz/50g sugar

Trim the sprouts, sprinkle with salt and leave overnight. Next day, rinse well under the cold tap. Drain well and pack into clean dry jars. Bring the vinegar, spices and sugar to the boil. Boil for 10 minutes and pour hot over the sprouts. Cover with a cloth until cold and cover with airtight lids. Do not use metal lids as vinegar will rust them. This is an unusual and good pickle and should be eaten within 2 months. Good with cold meats.

⋙⋙ November ⋘⋘

On the first of November if the weather hold clear,
An end of what sowing you do for the year

November sky is chill and drear,
November leaf is red and sere

NOVEMBER, WITH its dark days, the fogs and cold wet weather, can be a miserable time in the garden, but the bright foliage of golden and variegated evergreens does much to offset the general drabness. We look forward to the springtime coming. If you have the room in your garden, plant a shrub of *Prunus triloba,* which produces a profusion of small, double pink flowers in late March or early April. It is ideal for small gardens, and by cutting flowering branches back to three or four buds after flowering, it can be kept to a reasonable size.

Talking of planting, I always think that this is the best time to plant fruit trees and bushes; that is, if the soil is fit to stand on. If soil conditions are unsuitable, just make a hole in the corner of the garden, put them in and cover (this is what we call heeling-in your plants). Once you have your site ready, soak the roots thoroughly and set them firmly at the same depth as they were previously growing. Dig a hole large enough to take the full root spread, and break up the bottom soil. Now put your stake in so that you avoid damage to the roots. Cover with a little soil. I also like to put some good rotted mulch in, then more soil. Firm round the roots. Completely refill the hole and firm again. Keep an eye on the trees and never let them dry out in hot weather.

November is a good time to start pruning apples and pears; as soon as the leaves have fallen. A general tidying-up programme can now be undertaken, especially in the rock garden and pools.

Protect doubtfully hardy plants like some of the fuchsias (never cut down your fuchias, by the way – leave until late spring as the frost will get down to the crown more easily if the tops are taken off), by covering them with existing peat; also agapanthus, kniphofia (red hot pokers) and arum lilies. Protect the blooms of Christmas roses by placing two bricks either side of the plants, with a piece of glass over the top. This will help to keep water and snow off the flowers; also put a few slug pellets around the crowns. After the frost has blackened the dahlias, cut them down to 4–5in, lift and shake off the soil, wash in a weak solution of Jeyes Fluid and put them upside down to dry for about ten days. I stand them on the greenhouse bench, then store in peat or old contents of dry grow-bags, in a frost-free place. If the frosts are severe, do keep off the lawn, as it will be damaged by simply walking over the frosted grass, leaving footprints that turn brown. Don't leave your savings of seeds like broad beans, runner beans, peas, or even shallots in an outside shed where mice can get at them. I lost a lot of mine a few years ago when I stored the seeds in plastic boxes and the mice ate through the boxes. They will even eat shallots out of the seed trays.

When tidying up the flower borders, take a few crowns of lily-of-the-valley, pot up and stand in the cool greenhouse. You will get some nice early flowers in spring – could be an ideal present for Mothering Sunday.

Another task is repairing and repainting fences. One point I would like to mention – if you use creosote, be careful. If plants are growing nearby, a few drops will kill them, even the fumes will do so. (I once knew a chap who painted his greenhouse with creosote and for years his plants died as soon as the heat from the sun reached them; the fumes are so strong.) There are plenty of preservatives for fences which will do no harm to plants or shrubs.

When early chrysanthemum plants have finished flowering, the stems should be cut down to within 6in of soil level, to the part called the 'stool'. Shake out of pots or fork up if in the garden, and remove most of the soil. Treat them in the same manner as dahlias, steeping in a weak solution of Jeyes fluid. The stools should then be stood upright in boxes (old tomato trays) as close to one another as possible in a layer alternatively of soil and peat, making sure you put a name tag on each variety. The boxes can then be placed in a frame or cold greenhouse protected from frost. These will give you cuttings the following February or March.

As soon as the sharp frosts appear empty outside water tanks, as they will split if any water is left in them to freeze. Also remove water fountains and pumps from pools. A couple of tips I was given are to place an old tennis ball in the pool or take a plastic lemonade bottle and half-fill with hot water, place on the surface ice and refill with very hot water in severe frosty conditions. This allows oxygen and air to circulate for fish. Scrub out watering cans and leave upside down under cover – it's surprising how diseases can build up in your watering cans through the year.

If there be ice in November to bear a Duck,
There be nothing after but sludge and muck

Tender subjects like shrubs exposed to the winter for their first season will need some protection. A circle of wire netting loosely packed with old straw or bracken will help to keep frost off; or you can wrap them round with old polythene bags – it will all help.

Towards the end of November bring those spare crowns of rhubarb into the greenhouse for forcing. Take roots and stand them close together in a deep box under the greenhouse staging. Pack soil or old peat between them and cover with boards. You must give them absolute darkness, water moderately and try to keep the temperature at 50°F. Don't worry if the temperature does drop, you will still get nice rhubarb at a lower temperature. Keep an eye on tuberous begonias and gloxinias to ensure that there is no sign of disease. It's worth checking gladioli and dahlia tubers as well, and, if necessary, dust with a fungicide. Roses with a great deal of top growth can be trimmed back to avoid windrock; you can soon lose a rose if the wind keeps rocking it about, as a hole will form and become filled with water. Frost then sets in and the plant will die from the wet and icy conditions. Full pruning can be completed in the spring.

At the end of this month, I like to cut some shrubs, bringing branches into the house and placing them in water in a warm room to obtain early flowers for Christmas; such as *jasminum nudflorum*, forsythias, viburnum *bodnantense* and *fragrans*. Last but not least, a few pieces of my Contorta hazel or hazel corkscrew which has extraordinary twigs with catkins, (I love to see this tree in March, it just hangs with catkins, but the birds soon pull them off). It is often called 'Harry Lauders Walking Stick Tree'.

Runner bean trenches can be prepared now. My brother digs mine out, leaving it open all the winter months while I put in any garden waste – you would be surprised what goes in my trench. It does pay however, as I get some very good beans. Runner beans have hungry roots, they can take all the food and water you like to give them.

Ruby's Sweet & Savoury Sausage Stuffing

1lb/500g sausage meat
1 small onion
1 small apple
2 heaped tablespoons sultanas
2 heaped tablespoons breadcrumbs
2 heaped tablespoons sage & onion stuffing mix
salt & black pepper

Slice and cube onions and apples; mix all ingredients together, press into greased and bottom lined 1lb loaf tin. Cover with foil. Bake in hot oven Gas No6/ 400°F(200°C) for 35 minutes. Remove foil and leave for further 5 minutes. Serve hot with poultry or sliced cold.

⋙ December ⋘

December takes away everything and returns nothing

WITH THE REBIRTH of the sun at Christmas, the New Year opens up the promise of a new gardening year. Holly sprigs were exchanged as symbols of friendship. They were also symbols of eternal life and reputed to have many medicinal values. Sometimes a sprig was kept in the house to carry the good luck forward into the coming year. When we get a fine day in winter, we often say that it's a borrowed day which will have to be paid back later!

We all go into the garden to cut evergreens for our homes and churches etc at this time of the year. Do stand and look at the shrubs for a few minutes. Try and cut branches carefully so that you don't spoil the shape of the shrub. When you get your Christmas tree, and are planting it in a pot, do give it a good drink before bringing it into the house. Spray it with aerosol called 'N-Save', this will help prevent moisture loss and stop the needles dropping. I also use this spray on evergreens which I use for fresh, green arrangements over the festival period. It is a wise precaution to check over and remove the nets on your fruit-cages before the snows arrive, as the weight of snow in a heavy fall is likely to tear them.

Onion seed can be planted this month. Enthusiasts sow exhibition onion seed from the middle of December, some even sow on Boxing Day! A temperature of 55°F is required. Once the seedlings have germinated, they must be pricked out at the crook stage. This is when the first leaf is still half bent. I prick my plants out into small pots. Leeks for exhibition may also be planted out in the same way. Do send for your seeds as soon as possible, as some seed firms run out of the new and favourite varieties. If you get your onion sets, take them out of the small net bags, lay in seed trays and keep them in a cool place. It's handy to take up a few parsnips, swedes, leeks and a stick of Brussels sprouts. Dig a big hole in the garden, put the vegetables in and cover with old sacks or mats. Then, if the weather is bad and the ground is frosty, they are ready as you need them.

Where the wind blows on Christmas Eve,
There it will stay until May Eve

Sow successive sowings of mustard and cress, it will soon come up, even if you put some on a piece of damp kitchen paper – you will be surprised at how quickly it grows. Check seed trays and pots, giving them a good old spring clean! I like to get all my garden labels in and wash them with soap pads to get off all the old writing and names of plants. It is nice to have all your equipment ready for the new season.

Ivy and virginia creeper growing over the house or walls can be trimmed back around the window frames and away from the gutters, but this work will depend on the weather. Tool sheds will need an annual check, cleaning tools and wiping them over with an oily rag. Throw out any old bottles or tins with lost labels. Make sure that insecticides and garden chemicals are put into a frost-free shed. A grand job to do on a frosty day is to get the rest of the land dug, wheeling in your farmyard manure on to the land, leaving it in heaps until you are ready to use it. Leave the soil in large clumps, the frost will do more good than you can.

Check out fuchsias and pelargoniums, don't let them dry out completely. Bulbs which you planted for Christmas flowering should be ready for bringing into the house. The shoots want to be about 2in above the soil. If the weather and soil conditions are right, you can sow broad beans, such as the variety 'Aquadulce', and some round-seeded peas. But keep your eye out for the mice.

When pruning is completed, spray all fruit trees with tar oil, but do not apply to frosted trees. Give a good drenching to kill aphids, moths etc.

Try to get the children interested in growing some plants from the pips of fruit like oranges, grapefruit, lemons, dates, grapes or even apples. Once you get them interested, they might think about having gardens of their own – they are tomorrow's gardeners!

If you wish to make some cheap flower arrangements for Christmas, here is my way of using green ivy from the hedgerow. Take a nice, long spray of ivy and paint the edges with white blanco shoe whitener (the stuff that you use to clean children's plimsolls). Then take some glitter and shake it on the white edges of the ivy. You can also paint poppy seed heads in the same way, using a paint spray of different colours. I use the seed heads of montbretia too; they look so pretty sprayed gold and silver – but of course, the seed heads must be dry (I pick mine in October or November and hang them up in the shed to dry). Another seed to use is the common teasle – I put mine in a bucket upside down in some bleach, and this gets them a nice creamy colour. By the way, I grow teasles 'Dipsacus' (used in the textile industry for raising the nap on woollen cloth) in my flower borders. Cones are another useful decorative aid to use at Christmas, painted in different colours, but you will need to wire them. Children will love them; you can make little animals like owls and mice by sticking felt on them.

If you can't get a Christmas tree, find a twig or branch out of the hedgerow. Spray or paint it white or silver. You can tie heads of dried flowers on like helichrysum or small beech nut cases, sprayed red or green, or even acorn nut cases – but be sure to wire the cases first. There are a great variety of things which can be put on your tree to make it pretty. Another homely but useful decoration is the chinese lantern (*Physalis*), its orange lanterns hanging from 3 to 4ft stems. I like to cut along the ribs of the pointed lantern with sharp scissors, then pull back the petals to form a beautiful open flower; it looks like a large open rose. This method is better than just drying the stem, pulling off the leaves and having the lanterns suspended from the stems.

Mistletoe – myths and traditions

Ancient belief held that this plant was germinated by seeds contained in bird droppings. Hence the origin of the word probably

Summer in winter

came from the German word 'mist', meaning dung. As an old medieval writer put it, 'The thrush shiteth out the mistel berries'.

Mistletoe has been regarded as mysterious and sacred from the earliest times. In the pagan era as a bestower of life and fertility, a protection against poisons, illness and evil spirits, and also as an aphrodisiac. It was a great cult of the Druids. In the early Middle-Ages, it was the custom to hang a sprig of mistletoe over the house and stable doors to ward off witches and evil spirits. This, in conjunction with the English custom of those days (reported upon by many foreign visitors as being unique) to kiss everybody without fail upon arrival and departure, soon started the tradition. And when connected to old fertility rites from Greek Saturnalia and myths of Celtic and Anglo-Saxon customs, it soon evolved into present day practice.

Walnut Liquer

4oz/100g walnuts
4fl oz/114ml vodka
16fl oz/500ml white wine
3oz/75g sugar

Put the ingredients in a liquidizer and mix well. Pour into a jar and shake each day for a week. Strain (using the nuts for a cake or sweet). Put strained liquid with white wine and sugar. Mix well and keep for a week – if you can! Good Luck and Cheers!

Special Roast Parsnips

Many people just put a few parsnips around the Sunday joint but try using a few spices and it will add a little extra bite!

1½lb/¾kg peeled parsnips
2–3oz/75g dripping
2 teaspoons brown sugar
A good pinch of cayenne pepper
Ground cinnamon
Salt and pepper
Grated rind of one orange

Cut parsnips lengthways, removing woody core. Add to a pan of boiling, salted water and parboil about 4–6 minutes. Drain well. Heat roasting tin, add the parsnips and sprinkle over the sugar, spices, grated orange rind, salt and pepper, and roast in a hot oven 425°F (220°C) or Gas No7 for about 45 minutes, giving them a turn from time to time.

An old lady gave me this recipe. She told me that when she was in service, the master of the house liked his parsnips cooked in this way.

Garden Flowers

More and more people are going back to growing the old cottage garden plants and as I go to the Chelsea Flower Show each year, I notice that there is a turning back to cottage garden type flowers. One is asked 'Does it cost a lot?' You might think that planting in profusion is an expensive way of creating a garden. I suppose that it would be if you went out and bought all your plants at once to fill the borders. The best plan is to look around for Womens Institute markets, they are usually indoors and often have good plants at reasonable prices, well potted and labelled, and much cheaper than at the nurseries, (but perhaps I should not say that!)

When visitors come to see my garden their first reaction is to remark that every bit of space is used. My plants are grown in walls, old chimney pots, old boots, wine bottles and even old drainpipes. I then get a nice splash of colour at all heights. Years ago cottage gardens were unplanned – the rule was to have a wide border alongside a straight path edged with lavender or chives. I remember my father used to grow candytuft (*Iberis umbeiiata*) down our path; and also grew hollyhocks, aquilegia, bellis perennis daisy, canterbury bells, calendula (marigold), cornflower, larkspur, godetia, sweet peas and last but not least, his favourite the gaillardia. Once you have established a basic planting and get to know the heights of plants, you can soon adapt the cottage garden. But do remember to try and keep your garden simple and avoid fussy shapes for beds.

Another good idea is to grow vegetables in your flower garden. Oh yes – I have been growing them in patches in my borders for a number of years. For instance, I have Jerusalem artichokes growing at the back, plus a few runner beans. Some clumps of asparagus are also suitable and very decorative. My father used to have asparagus growing near the linen post so it could be tied to the post as it grew, then the fern was used as foliage to go with the sweet peas. It was never used as a vegetable in my childhood days. At the front of the border, plant a few patches of red beet, red chard and parsley and one of my old favourites, ornamental cabbage (you can leave these in all winter).

Herbaceous perennials are the most useful plants to have in the garden. Although there are hardy perennials for practically all sites and situations, mixed beds and borders need at least a moderate amount of sun and ideally some shelter from the strongest winds. Broadly speaking, herbaceous perennials go on year after year but die down either completely or to the crown of leaves for the winter, to start into new growth the following spring. A properly maintained border is a never-ending job. Digging in plenty of good muck, dividing, planting, staking, dead-heading, forking, fertilising, spraying – at the end of all these tasks, you can then have some cut flowers for the house. On the other hand it is not as bad as it seems, the majority of garden owners today just have a mixed border of shrubs and annuals, with herbaceous perennials mixed in the back somewhere. Most houses built today have only a small open-plan garden, pocket handkerchief size lawn with space for a few annuals around the outside.

I think one of the nicest things in gardening is growing your perennials from seeds. You do have to wait eighteen months or so for the plants to flower, but it does give that extra little bit of satisfaction. I will give you a list of some of the flowers which I grow, not just country-cottage types, but flowers which I need when I do church wedding flowers or special flower arrangements. Sometimes I don't need flowers – you can get wonderful effects with just foliage of many variegations. Here are some different varieties, including foliage plants:

Acanthus mollis or Bear's Breeches. A herbaceous perennial for the back of the border which will grow 3–4ft high.

Achillea or Yarrow (Gold Plate). This will grow in poor soil but likes the sun, and will be 2–3ft in height. The sparrows love eating the foliage so I cotton my plants as they start to grow in the spring.

Alchemilla or Lady's Mantle. Grows 12–18in. I would not be without this plant; to see the 'early dew' sparkling on the leaves is a wonderful sight as the leaves form a cup shape and water drops form in the middle. (However, this plant will seed all over the garden!)

Aquilegia or Columbine. Grows 4in to 2ft. There are many species of this flower. They are fairly short-lived but seed all over the garden. The dwarf plants are very pretty and make nice rock plants.

Artemisia. The button-shaped yellow flowers are insignificant but the leaves are a silvery grey, quite aromatic and the foliage has a feathery look. Grows 12–18in.

Arum italicum (Pictum). This would be another plant for me to take on my desert island. The handsome leaves are tough and this lovely form of 'Lords and Ladies' thrusts up its 12in tall spears of glossy green, cream and marbled leaves in late November through to the following summer. The flower is nothing to talk about, just a modified leaf with a poker stem in the middle and is seen in late August. After the leaves have died down, red berries appear on the stems, but do remember that they are poisonous! I think they are the flower arranger's dream when there is a shortage of foliage. It would be best if you have a friend who could supply you with a few berries, but be prepared to wait before you have full-sized leaves to use for your foliage arrangements. Sometimes the seeds will lay dormant for twelve months before germinating.

Aruncus or Goat's Beard. Another of my favourite plants, grows to 5ft in my garden. It likes a damp spot and is very effective near a pool. Visitors often ask if it is astilbe as its flower is very much like that of astilbe. Cream flowers in June and the attractive large, light-green leaves are composed of 5–7 lanceolate leaflets.

Astrantia or Masterwort. Height 24in. These unusual dainty flowers come in shades of pink, green and red and they love a shady border. The variegated leaves of some forms are a joy to have in the garden in the spring.

Ballota pseudodictamnus. Another plant grown for its foliage; it has grey wool-like leaves. It is a low growing, fairly hardy plant which will grow in poor soil and likes plenty of sun.

Chrysanthemum maximum or Shasta Daisy. Grows 2–3½ft. We call this plant Esther Read. At one time it was to be found in most cottage gardens, but now it's a job to find in any nursery. It is very useful to plant at the back of a border.

Delphinium. There are over 250 species of these lovely flowers. Three years ago I sowed seeds from a mixed packet and now have some lovely hybrids, all tints of blue and purple. Do watch out in the spring as slugs love the shoots. Grows 4–5ft.

Digitalis or Foxglove. Grows 3–4ft. A flower to remind one of a real cottage garden. They prefer dappled shade, but I find that they will grow in sun. The hybrids are beautiful plants; colours include cream, pink, apricot and even 'spotted' varieties. Bees love them!

Dianthus barbatus or Sweet William. Most people are surprised when I tell them that the Sweet William is from the dianthus family. My father used to grow rows and rows of this sweetly scented flower, with colours of crimson, scarlet or pink-edged with a brilliant white eye. I remember a stall holder describing them as a best seller when Sweet Williams were in season, he said ladies liked them for 'putting on graves'. In the book *The Language of Flowers* they are called the flower of gallantry. At one time, Sweet William was found growing on the hills of Normandy, west of Dieppe, so I think that the description fits it very well. There are many species of the family; one variety from the Thompson & Morgan catalogue called 'Roundabout' will flower from June to October. If sown in early spring it makes a nice edging plant as it only grows to a height of 6ins.

Dianthus caryophyllus or Carnation Pinks. The rich, spicy fragrance of the clove carnation is something you don't forget in a garden. This flower was cultivated in English gardens in the reign of Edward III and was used to give a spicy flavour to wine – this I can well believe!

The carnation's little cousin, the pink, is called the 'God of Wisdom'; it signifies pure and ardent love. The times I get asked where you can get the variety 'Mrs Simpkin', as you don't see it in catalogues these days are innumerable. A great favourite many years ago, I am pleased to say that it is coming back into fashion again. Mrs Simpkin has large white cabbage-like blooms borne on 12in stems above silvery green foliage, and of course, an almost overpowering perfume.

I also like the new and much improved Lace Pinks, ideal for rockery or borders. A show variety called Doris is another personal favourite – the double blooms of salmon pink with a dark eye are sweetly scented. I could go on and on, they are all so pretty.

Echinops or Globe Thistle. These perennial flowers, blue and globular, are very striking – the leaves being thistle-like. They are long-lasting and make big plants.

Erynging or Sea Holly. Grows 2–4ft. Another highly popular plant and now there are so many lovely strains getting about. I like to see the sun on the leaf; it has a glistening metallic sheen and is excellent for winter decorating.

Euphorbia. A poor soil border plant with very pretty green heads or bracts with petal-like appearance. I like *Wulfenii* (4ft) which is very good for cutting. Also I grow *Polychroma* (18in high). This has bright yellow 3in wide heads of bracts in early April. *Euphorbia lathyrus* is reputed to make soil unattractive to moles but I have never found this in my garden; it sets seeds freely.

Gaillardia or Blanket Flower. Grows 1½ to 2½ft. Broad petalled daisy flowers, mostly yellow and red in colour – a good cut flower. There is a good double mixed variety available.

Geum. This is another flower which was planted a lot in old-time cottage gardens. During recent years, many fine varieties have been introduced and I think that no garden should be without geums. Most people will know 'Lady Stratheden' (yellow) and 'Mrs Bradshaw' (red). These grow to heights of 18 to 24in tall and bloom from June to August. What I specially like are some of the dwarf varieties which I have seen growing in Beth Chatto's garden at Elmstead Market, Colchester. Beth has the most lovely flowers and shrubs, many in unusual varieties which you will find in her fascinating catalogue. Once you have read this unique publication you will want to visit her exquisite Haven of Peace.

Gypsophila (Paniculata). Bristol Fairy was the one which my Dad had in our cottage garden. This was cut and used with sweet peas and garden pinks, and sold in bunches at the gate. Sometimes it is called 'Baby's Breath' as it is so light and has tiny, lace flowers in pinnacles, often tinged with pink – I can see why it has this name. The best soil for growing this plant is a chalky mixture. The established root can be up to 2ft long (like a parsnip) and I find that they don't like being moved. This perennial can easily be grown from seed. I also dry this flower and use it a lot in flower arranging. I just tie small bunches and hang them up in the outside shed, then when making dried flower arrangements I fill in the spaces with gypsophila.

Helleborus. Once again, if I was put on a desert island, these plants would be a must to take. You start early in January with the *Helleborus foetidus.* The little, green, bell-like flowers edged with red hang down in clusters on pale green bracts. The leaves are fan-shaped rather like ten fingers spread out and I use the leaves all the year round for flower arrangements, as they stand up to being put in water, (stand in a bucket of water and immerse for 12 hours or so). The flowers are cut individually and the stems held in boiling water for one minute to seal them. *Helleborus corsicus* is a much larger plant, the leaves growing in three segments like claws. The flowers are more like small cups growing on erect stems with the plant spreading to 3ft or more. If you are lucky, you can pick flowers all through spring. Even with no flowers, the helleborus is a joy to have in the garden with its contrasting green hues.

Helleborus Orientalis or Lenten Rose. The colours are very pretty, ranging from pink to shades of purple, with spotted throats on some. I also have the variety called *Atrorubens,* which is similar to *Orientalis* but has a much darker flower – more purple in colour with lovely yellow stamens. The above-named two varieties have handsome foliage which looks good in the border for the rest of the year. All the helleborus like a rich soil in part shade, with plenty of farmyard manure dug into the soil. They may be grown from seed but, again, may take a year to germinate. A good tip – never throw away a pan of seed if it has not come up in 4–5 months. Some seeds take 12 to 18 months to germinate, so label and keep until some signs of life are observed.

Lathyrus or Sweet Peas. Another exquisite flower and one grown years ago in every cottage garden, in either perennial or annual form. My late father-in-law was so proud to have a sweet pea in his buttonhole by early Whitsun. Come to think of it, most of the country gardeners had a flower in their buttonholes, just to show off their first garden flower of the season, as well as to make a talking point in the local pub! Getting down to growing the sweet pea is easy; but you must remember one little chap who likes sweet pea seeds, and that is the mouse. When sowing in the garden, or in pans in the greenhouse, holly leaves help to keep him at bay. Another job which I do, is to soak the seed for 24 hours before sowing, as they have an extremely hard coating. If you sow in October, in frame or greenhouse, you should have some nice strong plants to put out in early spring. These plants will need plenty of light; also pinch out the growing tips to make the plants bush out into strong plants.

There are many varieties from which to choose, starting with dwarf – 1ft to 18in – Snoopea, Sweetheart, Bijou. I find that these varieties are good for growing in hanging baskets and containers. For the tall growing ones, you can obtain any colour under, or in, the rainbow, but a favourite of mine is the bi-colour called 'Wiltshire Ripple', a rich, claret red on a white background, introduced by Thompson & Morgan several years ago. With the Everlasting Sweet Pea, the above-mentioned firm introduced a blue-coloured variety in 1986, called *Nervosus*. This has blooms of powder blue, is a strong grower on my soil and goes well with a pink variety called *Latifolius*, which also grows well for me, covering my sheds all through the summer months.

Lavatera arborea 'variegata' or Tree mallow. This is another plant of which I have grown very fond. I have one planted in an old pot, a 'by-gone' which cottagers used for storing bread. Not fully hardy in cold areas, the tree mallow's leaves have white, mottled marking and are soft and velvety to touch. Cuttings can be taken easily. This is a nice specimen to grow near a wall or fence with a little bit of shelter.

Lupinus or Lupin. I cannot understand why more people don't grow lupins; the Russell Lupin makes a truly majestic addition to the borders and I feel nothing can beat it for colour. George Russell was a handyman-gardener who loved growing lupins and spent a lifetime hybridising the superb strain at his garden in York. Hours were spent in crossing varieties, but not, alas in keeping records! He obtained seed from all over the world. In 1935, 1,500 varieties were grown in his garden. Eventually, his seed was all sold to Messrs Baker of Codsall, near Wolverhampton. George was awarded the MBE in 1951 in his ninety-fourth year, for service to horticulture. Another 'salt of the earth' type – a good man, we say.

I sow lupin seeds in a pan in late spring, then pot up and stand in a frame for the summer and plant them in their permanent position in late autumn. Plants should be split up every three years. Try growing variety 'Dwarf Lulu' – 2ft which is ideal for small gardens. Do dead-head to get a second crop of flowers. The 'Band of Nobles' has much improved in colours over the years.

Macleaya or Plume Poppy. You most probably will not see this flower in small gardens as it does take up 'a rare lot of room' (large space). The roots are invasive and spread out to Kingdom Come! But I do like to see it growing at the back of my borders. When in full growth, the plant will climb to 8–9ft high with pretty white plumes of flowers in July/August, above dense mounds of rounded bronze leaves.

Onopordum or Scotch Thistle. I expect one would say 'fancy growing thistles', but this one is extra special. Once again, a plant which grows best in the back of borders, towering above all the other flowers as it will reach up to 9–10ft, with broad, silver-grey leaves and pale purple flowers appearing in July and August. Flower arrangers love this plant, in spite of its prickly leaves. The seedlings will turn up all over the garden. My visitors enjoy seeing onopordum, although it is a thistle.

Paeonia or Peony. Dr D. G. Hessayen called this flower the aristocrat of the herbaceous perennial world. I must agree with him, as they look to me like royal flowers, with their brilliant colours. In my father's time, you would have the common peony *Officinalis* growing in cottage gardens, with the bright red colour shining in the borders under the windows. Now there are many varieties ranging from perennials to tree peonies, grown for their handsome flowers and attractive foliage. Again, the foliage is used throughout the summer for filling in on flower arrangements. One thing the peony doesn't like, is being transplanted. Also don't try to divide clumps or you will get no flowers for two or three years. Try and raise some from seed (if saving your own seed, sow right away for better germination) – they will take about a year or more to germinate.

Papaver or Poppy. Several seed strains have come on the market over the years. At one time in my garden, I had just the poppy *orientale* called 'Mrs Perry'. Then I saw 'Perrys White' in Beth Chatto's garden and I just had to have one. It looks so fine growing near my delphiniums. Once you have poppies in the garden you will never be without them, as every bit left in the ground will grow. Annual species are just as pretty; try growing 'Pink Chiffon', the seed pods make lovely dried heads. 'Iceland Poppy' is a short-lived perennial usually grown as a biennial. 'Oregon Rainbows', introduced from Oregon, USA, have a fine bloom 6–8in across and contrasting colours, peach pink to cream picotees. When I first planted these, I was amazed at the height and strong-growing plants. If sown in heat in February in the greenhouse, you will get flowers in the middle of the summer.

Phlomis or Jerusalem Sage. Not all gardeners would grow the phlomis, but I like the way the yellow flowers grow in clusters down the stems in between the sage-like leaves. *Phlomis fruticosa* is the one I grow, making a shrub of 3ft in height, spreading 2ft and flowering in July. This plant likes a sunny position. After the flowers have dropped, I like to use the stems later, for drying.

Phlox. One of the biggest collections of phlox I have seen grown are at Bressingham Gardens in Diss, Norfolk. Twenty-seven varieties are listed in their fine catalogue. Easy to grow, but they like a moist soil. I don't think a herbaceous border should be without them. I grow mine in mixed clumps, dividing every other year, discarding woody parts and replanting only the outside parts of old clumps. The plant grows to 2½–3ft in height. Flowers are all colours, borne in massive pyramidal pinnacles on stems, flowering July to September.

Physalis (Chinese Lantern) or Winter cherry. This is also known as 'Bladder Herb'. and last, but not least, 'Strawberry Tomato'. So many names for this flower – more useful in the winter for drying than in the summertime in the garden, I feel it will grow in most soils. The roots of the variety *Franchetii* can become too invasive (just like growing the herb mint), so plant it in a corner where it will not overtake other plants. You will need some sun to ripen the lanterns. Cut the stems in September–October, tie in bunches and dry off. The summer flowers look like white stars, eventually turning into fine orange lanterns.

Physostegia or Obedient Plant. This is another plant I would take on my island. My first plant was the white form called 'Summer Snow' and it looks so fine growing near my *Perovskia.* It is a blue spire, shrubby perennial. Last year, I planted *Variegata* form which has very pretty foliage. The plant gets its name of 'Obedient' from the fact that, when picked, the florets on the stems remain in a set position. They can be grown in most soils but not where it gets too dry. 'Rose Bouquet' is another good grower, all plants growing 2½–3ft tall.

Polemonium or Jacobs Ladder. This is another old-fashioned flower. It has pretty, little blooms and appears in my garden when there are not many other blooms, in early May. The name 'Jacobs Ladder' was given because the leaves are much like a ladder, also it is one of our oldest garden plants. I feel that the foliage is just as pretty as the flowers and once you have a plant you will find that it seeds itself freely. You will need to split up the roots in autumn or spring as the clumps get quite large. The flowers grow to about 2ft and are bright blue in colour. There is also a white variety.

Polygonatum or Solomons Seal. This flower is loved by flower arrangers and is also one of my favourites. I look at this plant with its arching sprays of foliage and little white flowers hanging in clusters down the stems and they make me think of little baby's shoes. *Polygonatum multiflorum variegatum* is a rare bonus, with its foliage of cream and green and this variety grows to 3–3½ft, a little taller than the common Solomon Seal. All polygonatum like shade, and the roots have rhizomes which should be split up in October. I like to divide my plants every third year. Give them plenty of farmyard manure – they love it!

Polygonum or Knotweed. Some people will call the polygonum a weed, but if the right variety is chosen to suit the garden, I am sure that they will be satisfied. For instance, I grow a deep-red variety called 'Donald Lowndes'. It produces poker-like flowers between July and October, 1½ to 2ft high with nice, bronzed foliage. All polygonums can be invasive. A creeping variety called *vaccum-folium* has pretty, deep-pink spikes. These flowers will thrive in most soils, sun or shade and also dry very well.

Pulmonaria or Lungwort. I always look for the first flower to appear on my pulmonaria or 'Soldiers and Sailors' (another nickname), because then I know that winter is over. The well-known variety I have, called 'Saccharata' (also called 'Bethlehem Sage') has silver markings on the foliage, pinkish-mauve flowers and grows to about 1ft in height. Pulmonaria will grow in most soils. Once the flowers die, cut them down so that the foliage will make a fine garden-feature for the rest of the season.

Pyrethrum or Feverfew. I am going to say it once more – one of my much-loved flowers. This daisy-like flower comes out my garden when there is a shortage of flowers, and I do like to use it in pedestal arrangements round about May, in clumps of bright green foliage (much like carrot foliage) and flowers on stems of 12–18in long, red and pink with yellow centres. There are some fine doubles; 'Vanessa' is very good, with a large yellow centre. The pyrethrum likes a well-drained soil and the full sun. I would just like to say that, if you grow pyrethrums, do make sure that you remove flower stems once the blooms have finished – you will prolong the season, with a little bit of luck. A good cut flower and very easy to grow from seed.

Scabiosa (Scabious) or Pincushion Flower. Another excellent cut flower. I well remember my father growing rows of these plants across the garden. The blue *Caucasica* is still a good grower and the flowers keep coming from early summer till the first frosts appear. A white variety called 'Bressingham White' does well in my garden. There are some good annual scabious and the seed heads can be dried. Scabious grow on well-drained soil in full sun. Try and divide established clumps every third year.

Sisyrinchium or Rush Lily. You don't see this flower around much. It looks very striking in borders, with the yellow and white primrose-like flowers growing all the way up the stems. The leaves are sword shaped, rather like the iris family. The variety in my garden is called 'Striatum'. Flowers appear in June and July. Peat and leaf mould dug into the soil help to make it happy; also a sunny position.

Solidago or Golden Rod. Most cottage gardens have this plant; come to that, town gardens as well. With modern hybrids, gardeners will like to choose named species as there are varieties available which will reach 4 to 5ft tall, coming down to 1ft in height. One problem which I find is that Golden Rod will soon exhaust the soil and needs to be split up regularly. This plant makes me think of harvest festivals in our churches, with the golden yellow, arching, soft plumes, arranged with rose hips and dahlias – a lovely sight.

Try growing 'Mimosa'. It's tall but worth it for the fine plumes which come in late August. 'Golden Thumb' grows to just over 12in high if you require a short variety.

Tellima Grandiflora. You will guess as you read this book, that I love foliage of any description. Tellima is another of God's creations, with reddish, purple-flushed leaves, especially colourful in the dark months of winter. The flowers are on a thin stem rising out of the plant, small and pale green, like bells, changing to pink. Beth Chatto obviously thinks as I do. In her book *Plant Portraits,* she says of tellima: 'At its best when times are bad', as in her January notes she describes how this plant stands up to the winter weather. I find that these plants are good ground cover and easy to grow, in sun or shade.

Thalictrum or Meadow Rue. For those who value plants with graceful elegant foliage, these are the ones to grow in the border; a pleasant contrast to the heavy-leaved plants. Thalictrum's maidenhair fern appearance is a joy for the flower arranger. The variety *Diptorocarpum* (what a mouthful) bears heads of lavender flowers with large yellow stamens. Of all the varieties this would be the one I would choose. You will find that thalictrum grow in any reasonable soil; but remember that the one I have been talking about grows up to 5ft in height. I also grow *Speciosissimum* which grows 5 to 6ft high and has yellow flowers.

Trollius or Globe Flower. The little yellow Globe Flowers are ideal for colour in your garden in May. No, you don't need a bog to grow these interesting plants; as long as you can find a damp corner, they will grow. To look at the flower resembles a large buttercup. A lot of work has been done on the first Common Trollis and one can obtain very good hybrids like 'Canary Bird' or 'Lemon Queen', also an orange variety called 'Golden Queen'.

Verbascum Mullein. The verbascum are among the most hardy of plants. Like the species of *Bombyciferum,* the huge, felted leaves are more attractive than the tall spines of yellow flowers; but I must warn you that if you have a small garden, don't grow this variety as it will attain a height of 6–8ft. There are other species; one which I like is called 'Pink Domino', with pretty pink flowers. I save the long seed stems for drying and using in winter arrangements. Verbascum likes a well-drained soil and full sun, if this can be arranged. Easy to take cuttings or to grow from seed.

All the border plants I have mentioned are grown in my garden; also lots more, but one is unable to mention them all. I hope that this selection will provide a guide, and help if you are starting your first garden. Remember, my garden has had plenty of good farmyard compost over the years, so my plants grow taller and wider than varieties in the catalogues.

Annuals

These are plants which grow naturally and flower, seed and die within twelve months. Some examples are:–

Ageratum Blue Mink
Alyssum Little Dorrit
Amaranthus Love-lies-bleeding, Crimson and Green
Antirrhinum Little Darling, Sweetheart, Maximum mixed
Aster Milady, Cut and Come Again
Begonia Clips F^1
Begonia Semperflorens Fibrous Rooted, Lucia F^1
Brachycome Purple Splendour
Cabbage Ornamental Red and White Peacock
Calceolaria Midas F^1, Fothergillii

Candytuft Fairy Mixture
Chrystanthemum Annual Court Jester
Clarkia Royal Bouquet Mixed
Cobaea Scandens
Convolvulus Blue Flash
Cosmos Sea Shells
Impatiens Busy Lizzies, Futura Double Duet,
Blitz Double Rosette Mixed
Lobelia Blue Cascade, Snowball, Crystal Palace
Marigold Incas (African), Tiger Eyes (French) Honeycomb
Matricaria Tom Thumb, White Stars
Nasturtium Whirlybird, Alaska
Nicotiana Nick F^1, Lime Green
Osteospermum Starshine
Pansy Jumbo, Liverpool Festival, Queen of the Plants
Petunia Bouquet F^1 mixed, Cascade Resisto
Rudbeckia Goldilocks, Marmalade
Salvia Horminum, Clarissa, Blaze of Fire, Rodeo
Senecio Cineraria Silver Dust
Stocks Happistok
Sweet Pea Snoopea and old-fashioned varieties
Tagetes Lemon and Orange Gem, Starfire
Verbena Showtime, Vonosa
Zinnias Chippendale, Envy

These are just some of the annuals that I grow; also I do like to ring the changes with new varieties coming out each year.

Perennials

A perennial plant is one which lives for more than two years. They include trees, shrubs and plants which grow from bulbs, corms and tubers; in fact, all which are not annuals or biennials. Antirrhinums, petunias, wallflowers and some other plants are usually grown as annuals or biennials in gardens, but botanically may be true perennials.

Some gardening terms and their meanings:

Biennial A plant which grows from seed and which ordinarily requires two seasons to grow with second flowering, seeding and dying.

Calyx The outer set of perianth segments especially when green.

Corm A bulb-like corm is an underground stem stored with reserve food, (like gladiolus and cyclamen).

Cuttings Any portion of leaf bud stem removed from a plant and treated in such a way that it will form a new individual plant. I find this way one of the best to get new individual plants, and an easy way to obtain cheap plants. They also can be taken at all times of the year. Before the cuttings are inserted in a rooting medium they must be trimmed cleanly with a sharp knife. I have my pruning knife, given to me by one of my old neighbours, and this I really treasure as he first showed me how to prune roses with this knife. Stem cuttings should be cut immediately below a node or joint. Leaves, stalks and buds should be removed from the portion of the cutting to be inserted and the ends may be dipped in a root-prompting hormone substance. Cuttings will root successfully under conditions that supply them with adequate moisture, temperature and light. Softwood cuttings need a moist atmosphere in a closed propagating frame at an average temperature of 18°C (64°F) while half-ripe cuttings inserted in the same conditions will root in a temperature of about 16°C (59°F). Cuttings in closed propagating frames should be inspected and watered daily. If the weather gets very hot, cover tops with brown paper or newspapers. Soft cuttings propagated with bottom heat will root in 1–2 weeks; half-ripe cuttings take up to 4 weeks to form roots. Hardwood cuttings should always be taken in autumn and inserted outdoors – these cannot be expected to root until the following spring.

Deciduous A deciduous tree and shrub is one having leaves which persist only one season and fall in the autumn.

Evergreen A plant which retains its living foliage for at least a full year and never loses its leaves.

Everlasting A plant which has flower heads that retain much of the colour character after being cut and dried.

Foliage The leaves of any plant, also stems bearing only leaves.
Frond The leaf of a fern or palm.
Half hardy A half hardy plant is one which may be grown in the open air for part of the year, but must be lifted and protected in some way during the winter.
Hardy A hardy plant is one which is able to survive the average winter when grown in the open.
Herbaceous perennial A plant with a non-woody stem which dies down to the ground completely each winter but has a rootstock which remains alive throughout several years.
Herbaceous plant A plant that does not form a persistant woody stem; it may be annual, biennial or perennial.
Hybrid A plant derived from the interbreeding of two or more genetically distinct plants, usually two or more species.
Pricking out Taking the seedlings and putting them in seed boxes or trays (seed boxes are wooden boxes 16in by 12in). We use old tomato trays which can be bought from the greengrocer for a few pence, or trays which have contained grapes. You can buy plastic trays; these are rather smaller than the wooden ones but they will do just as well. Pricking out gives plants a better chance to grow as the box is filled with soil-less compost which is soaked as well. Mark holes in rows so that you can get 36 or 48 plants pricked out into the boxes (depending on the seedlings). Salvias and petunias need more room than say, marigolds or asters. Keep them growing till you think they are ready to plant out, then transfer them to a cold frame (this is a large wooden frame with a glass or plastic top) – moving the trays or boxes from the greenhouse to the frame to harden off. This gets your plants acclimatised to cooler weather.
Propagation The increase of plants by such techniques as budding, cutting, division, grafting and layering. Budding is chiefly used to propagate roses, (a well developed leaf bud with a sliver of bark attached is joined to an appropriate rootstock). Budding is carried out while the plants are in full growth – from mid-June until the end of August. One year old, well-rooted stem cuttings of old briar roses are suitable stocks for bush roses (we look for standard roses in the hedgerows in the autumn, dig them up and plant them so that the following summer we can bud them). The leaf bud of a

choice variety is inserted in a T-shaped incision in the bark of the stock and bound firmly with raffia. We bud our standard roses from 4 to 5ft from ground level. On bush roses the buds are inserted just below the soil level.

Seedling A plant produced from a seed as opposed to one propagated by grafting or other vegatative means.

Shrub A woody perennial, often many stemmed, or smaller structure than a tree and having no distinct trunk.

Summer flowers

Spray For flower show purposes, a spray is a branched flower with many flower heads on a main stem.
Standard A term applied to a tree or other plant with an upright stem of some length supporting a head like a fuchsia or heliotrope, chrysanthemum or pelargonium. (These are some ornamental plants grown as standards.)
Tender A tender plant is one which requires a favourable location or situation which may need some form of protection in winter.
Tuber A swollen, underground stem with buds and eyes from which new plants or tubers are produced, eg potatoes, dahlias and gloxinias.

There are many legends attached to plants which I, for one, find very interesting. It is nice to know how a plant comes to be called by a sometimes unpronounceable name, or if it has any uses other than that of reproducing and looking pretty in our gardens and vases. Here are some of the interesting facts attributed to flowers:

Achillea Named after the Greek hero Achilles who is supposed to have used a variety of achillea for treating wounds.
Amaranthus Named from the Greek amarantos, which means unfading.
Asclepias Named after the Greek god of medicine; though what he did with asclepsias, I would not know.
Carlina From Carlinus, Latin for Charlemagne, who is said to have cured his army of the plague with this plant.
Catananche From the Greek katanangke meaning a strong incentive; the plant has been used as a love potion in years gone by.
Echinops The globe thistle, a very apt, name, Echinos is Greek for hedgehog!!
Salvia From the Latin for safe or well, salvus. Some species have medicinal properties.
Scabiosa From the Latin scabies; certain species were supposed to be a cure for the disease of the same name.
Solidago From the Latin solido, to make whole; some solidago varieties are supposed to have curative powers.

Flowers for Drying

Talking to the plants? This is something I often do, but not for any scientific reason. I go into the greenhouse and say 'How are you today, my dears. Fair to middling?' I often talk to myself when I am in the greenhouse and I think that the plants can definitely feel your presence – whether you are for them, or not.

When we do get some sunshine, I feel the urge to start to sow my seeds in the greenhouse. My plan is always to get my bedding plants out by the end of May. One of my interests (already apparent) is flower arranging, so I like to grow a lot of everlasting flowers. I don't sow straight into the soil but prefer to sow in seed trays and then plant out into the soil at the end of May. They are so easy to grow and a joy to have in the winter months, but I must say at this stage that many people make the mistake of picking the flowers when the full colour is showing. I pick mine when you can just see the colour, then hang them upside down in small bunches in the outside shed – they need cool, dry conditions. I also experiment with other flowers which can be used for drying; believe me, you may be surprised at the varieties which can be dried. Here are a few examples:

Acanthus mollis (Bear's Breeches) Hardy perennial
Achillea family Hardy perennial
Alchemilla mollis Hardy perennial
Amaranthus Caudatus mixed Annual
Ammobium Annual
Anaphalis Hardy perennial
Asclepias Hardy perennial
Carlina Hardy perennial
Catananche Hardy perennial
Celosia Annual
Cynara Hardy perennial
Dipsacus (Teasel) Hardy biennial
Echinops (Globe Thistle) Hardy perennial
Eremurus Hardy perennial
Eryngium Hardy perennial

Gnaphalium Hardy perennial
Gomphrena Annual
Gypsophila Hardy perennial
Helichrysum Annual
Helipterum Annual
Larkspur Annual
Lavender Hardy shrub
Liatris Hardy perennial
Limonium (Statice) Annual
Lonas (Honesty) Annual
Molucella-lavis (Bells of Ireland) Annual
Montbretia (seed heads only) Hardy perennial
Nigella damascena (Love-in-a-Mist) Hardy perennial
Physalis (Chinese Lantern) Hardy perennial
Podolepis Annual
Rodanthe Annual
Salix (Pussy Willow) Hardy shrub
Salvia (Claryssa) Annual
Sedum Hardy perennial
Scabiosa (Stellata Drumstick) Annual
Solidago (Golden Rod) Hardy perennial
Xeranthemum Annual
Zea (Ornamental Maize) Annual

Grasses
Agrostis Nebulosa Cloud Grass
Avena Sterillis Animated Oats
Briza Maxima Quaking Grass
Briza Minor Little Quaking Grass
Coix Lacryma-Jobi Job's Tears
Cortaderia Selloana Silver Pampas Grass
Cortaderia Selloana Rose Shades Pampas Grass
Cortaderia Tulvida Black Pampas Grass
Eragrostis Elegans Love Grass
Eriophorum Latifolium Cotton Grass
Festuca Glauca
Hordeum Jubatum Squirrel Tall Grass

Koeleria Glauca Blue Meadow Grass
Lagarus Ovatus Hares Tail Grass
Melica Ciliata Pearl Grass
Melica Transsilvanica Rosy Pearl Grass
Milium Effusum Aureum Bowles Golden Grass
Panicum Violaceum
Pennisetum Longstylum
Phalaris Canariensis
Polypogon Monspeliensis
Setaria Glauca Foxtail Grass
Stipa Pennata Feather Grass
Tricholaena Rosea
Triticum Spelta

Preserving with glycerine is a good way for long-lasting foliage and flowers. The plant material must be treated while it is still absorbing moisture and before any parts begin to dry, as the glycerine must be taken by the stem and carried to every part of the cutting in order to give complete preservation. I love to do copper beech foliage and seed heads in this way.

Recipe

Pour into a jar 1 part glycerine and 2 parts of hot water. Stir well. The mixture may be used over and over again.

Herbs

More and more people are discovering the benefits to be had from using plants, flowers and herbs to improve the quality of their health. Yet the healing and beautifying properties of flowers and herbs were recognised by our ancestors hundreds of years ago. Many of today's more conventional medicines have their roots in ancient folklore.

Foxglove *(Digitalis)* is a widely acclaimed drug for treatment of heart ailments. Garlic was also a great favourite in past centuries as an antiseptic. It's ten times weaker than penicillin, but then it was all they had years ago! One can understand why our grandparents carried garlic cloves in their pockets – it had so many uses. I often get asked if the feverfew gives relief for migraine. Many severe headache sufferers are growing their own plants of feverfew. As a migraine comes on, you should pick a few leaves and eat them between slices of bread; it has a very bitter taste. You should eat two leaves a day if you are a migraine sufferer. However, with modern medicine you can buy products in liquid and tablet form which eliminate the bitter taste.

If you have an almond tree growing in your garden you can crush the leaves with some of the flowers, shells and even some of the bark, boil them together and add to your bathwater and they should help induce relaxation and sleep. Heather is another plant which you can steep in hot water and this should help with rheumatism; it also contains a natural disinfectant and is good for blemishes and spots. Even the nettle has its uses. I make nettle wine, and one can even cook the top leaves and eat them like cabbage. Nettle is pleasantly sweet and it helps anaemia and arthritis sufferers. We had a lady in our village who used to boil nettle leaves, add a few drops of eau-de-cologne and use it when rinsing her hair; she 'never had dandruff'. Even nettle roots can be boiled in water and the juice taken to relieve diarrhoea. I expect a lot of people would say they would rather have the diarrhoea!

Rosemary leaves and flowers infused in boiling water are a good cure for bad breath, and a good tonic for digestion. Comfrey is another valuable herb; it makes excellent ointments and, used externally, will help to heal fractures and ulcers. It can even be taken as a drink made from the crushed roots boiled in milk, or in the form of an infusion of the leaves. Years ago, comfrey was known variously as Cure-all, Knit-bone, Bone-set. With all these names there is little wonder that its prime use is to promote healing of fractures. Comfrey is one of the tallest members of the borage family (2–3ft). The flowers vary considerably in colour from purple-red to yellow to white. It also has nice, broad leaves. Fresh comfrey leaves can be cooked as a plain green vegetable like spinach, and are tastier if the cooked leaves are mixed with a good white sauce topped with grated cheese. I always say that you can make a good meal from the hedgerow as long as you know your plants.

Now I will give you a list of some of my favourite herbs and why I like them:

Borage is a tall hairy-leaved annual with vivid blue star-shaped flowers. It's a nice plant to have at the back of the border and whatever the weather, borage continues to bloom for many months of the year. Its leaves and flowers have a fresh cucumber flavour – the chopped leaves can be used in salads and the flowers in a fruit punch.

Horse radish is a hardy perennial with large floppy leaves, a bit like the dock leaf. I am often asked how to get rid of it from the garden as it has long roots; you think you have dug it all up and then it pops out of the earth once more. At one time it could be found at the road side, but it's a job to find it nowadays. I usually manage to buy some roots at our Womens Institute market in the autumn. I remember putting some in the food processor to grate – although it did the job well, when I took the lid off the strong aroma hit me and my eyes were watering for a long time afterwards. But what better can you wish for with that rib of beef for Sunday lunch? It wouldn't be the same without homemade radish sauce, none of your supermarket cream stuff! In the Middle Ages it was used to aid digestion and the crushed roots were used externally for aching joints. (Don't cook horse radish as it loses its pungency.)

Water cress is a hardy, aquatic perennial. It has small, shiny, rounded leaves which creep through the water and grow upright to about 9–12in high. The flavour of the leaves and stems, which are the edible parts, is strong and peppery and it is rich in iron and vitamin C. Its main uses are in salads and garnishes. Since it is unobtainable in the local shops, I grow land cress (or American cress). This is quickly maturing and much hotter in flavour. It is best eaten when young, hence sow every six weeks.

Mint – there is a big family of this herb with differences in leaf form, flavour and flowers, but all having square stems. The most important point to remember with mint if you wish to keep its fresh green leaves, is to remove the flowering spikes. Flavour varies tremendously from plant to plant. Good mints may deteriorate after years of planting in the same place. Rust diseases can soon spread as mints are very prone to this problem. The only cure is to dig up the affected plants and burn them, beginning again with new, healthy runners. There are far too many varieties to mention, but here is a list of the ones which I grow:–

Apple Mint *(Mentha rotundifolia)* This is a vigorous growing mint and is less prone to the rust disease. The flavour is like ripe apples. A variegated variety is available which flower arrangers like to use.

Spearmint *(Mentha viridis spicata)* One of the best to use when making mint sauce; it has a nice strong flavour.

Eau-de-cologne Mint *(Mentha citrata)* Sometimes called the orange mint; the leaves are good in cool drinks.

Peppermint *(Mentha piperita)* Has a lovely strong scent, and crops from this hybrid are now grown all over the world. The oil extracted from the plant contains menthol which is still used as a local analgesic for sprains, toothache and bruises. Peppermint oil is used for flavouring sweets and cakes.

Lemon Thyme *(Thymus citriodorus)* A nice, sweetly scented thyme, which I like to plant on a bank. The small leaves smell strongly of lemon and the bees love this plant. I use it for stuffings, and put a bunch in the water when boiling a chicken.

Marjoram *(Origanum Marjorana)* A perennial plant in warm climates, it has to be grown elsewhere as an annual. Grows about 1ft high with small leaves. Its cooking uses are excellent with meats, especially if making a meat loaf.
Rosemary *(Rosmarinus Officinalis)* This is a must in any garden, whether you grow herbs or not. An evergreen shrub, it can grow up to 6ft high, but is very slow growing. The leaves are short and narrow, and the flowers grow in crowded clusters of pale blue. Rosemary was traditionally used as a protector against spirits, fairies, lightning and injury, for success in enterprises and as a charm for lovers. It is also a symbol of constancy and was sometimes thrown into a coffin at a funeral. It is still used in the Queen's posy carried at the Maundy Day ceremony. Rosemary has many uses in the kitchen and in medicine and is effective as a moth repellant.
Sage *(Salvia Officinalis)* Another fine herb I would hate to be without in my garden. An old supersition was that 'if the sage bush thrives and grows, the master's not the master and he knows!' The symbol of domestic virtue:

He that would live for aye
Must eat Sage in May

This is an ideal plant for growing in containers, growing to a height of 2–4ft. The leaves are narrow and pale grey-green with a rough texture. I grow the purple sage (sometimes called black sage) for ornamental purposes, the flavour is not so good. Pork would not be the same without a good stuffing of sage and onions. It also makes a good mouthwash.
Bay *(Laurus nobilis)* was sacred to Apollo and Aesculapius, god of medicine. It was a plant associated with honour, fame and victory, and a great protector and healer. The Romans used bay as a favourite decoration in their houses and festivals. It was also used against withcraft, the devil, snake bite and thunder. The emperor Tiberius would crawl under the bed during thunderstorms and cover his head with bay leaves. Sweet bay, or bay laurel as it is sometimes known, is the name given to this perennial evergreen

shrub and is the only form of laurel used in cooking. You often see standard bay trees standing outside restaurants. Where the winters are likely to be severe, bring your bays in (I always stand mine in the cold greenhouse). You can pick the leaves throughout the year and they dry well. Bay is also one of the three herbs used in 'bouquet garni'. Poached fish is much improved with the use of bay leaves. Store a couple of leaves in your rice jar!!

Angelica *(Angelica archangelica)* This is a fine handsome plant to have in the garden. I like to place it at the back of the border as it grows up to a height of 6ft. It is supposed to bloom on St Michael's Feast of Apparition. Angelica used to be called the root of the Holy Ghost and once grew freely in London squares. It is extremely fragrant and was chewed during the Great Plague of 1665 to avoid infection. Cooks love this herb as the stems or leaf stalks can be candied, making that nice, green, candied angelica which we find on so many homemade cakes at country fetes and market stalls. Medicinally it has many uses including as a good cough syrup and for easing sore throats. Angelica tea is good for indigestion.

Balm Lemon *(Melissa officinalis)* Another herb of which I am very fond, and one which makes very good homemade wine (that's probably why I like it!) Culpeper wrote of balm:

> *It causeth the mind and heart to become merry,*
> *And driveth away all troublesome cares and thoughts*

Lemon balm rubbed in a new hive would make the bees settle in their new home. The herb comes from the Middle East where, in the past, it was taken as a refreshing tea. Lemon balm will grow very easily; it's a bit like mint – it soon spreads. In cooking it is good in stuffings and fruit cups.

Chives *(Allium achoenoprasum)* At one time you could see rows of chives edging cottage gardens. My father used to chop chives and mix them in with the chicken food. Another superstition is that if chives are planted around the apple tree your apples won't get 'scab'. The chive is much milder in flavour than the onion. It grows in clumps 12–16in high. Try not to let it keep its mauve flowers as it will lose its flavour. Chopped chives in egg dishes are very good; also use with cream or cottage cheese.

Fennel *(Foeniculum vulgare)* The fennel is a magnificent looking plant and I like to see it growing with the flowers. It sometimes grows up to 5ft tall with fine feathery leaves and yellow flowers, and has the flavour of sweet anise. Historically, fennel was used as a medicine – it was believed to strengthen the eyesight and cure an upset stomach. The ancient Greeks considered it a symbol of success. Fennel leaves have long been used for flavouring fish dishes, a traditional trick even in Culpeper's day. Florence fennel or finocchio is a variety which has an edible swollen leaf-base like celery. It needs a long, warm, growing season and plenty of moisture. The leaves and seeds can be used like garden fennel. I grow that bronze form of fennel as this dark foliage is so pretty with flowers and it makes a nice contrast in colour. As well as being used in fish dishes, the seeds can be ground or used whole to flavour bread. An infusion of fennel is a good treatment for inflamed eyes, also for those who suffer from cramp.

Well, I could go on and on writing about herbs, but these are just a few varieties which I like to grow and use.

Some Favourite Shrubs

Berberis
There is a tremendous range of this colourful shrub. For flower or foliage it takes some beating as the most useful shrub in my garden and I am always cutting it for flower arrangements. The *thunbergii* group has grown in numbers over the years. My *atropurpurea,* which has rich, bronzy-red foliage in spring and turns red in the autumn, looks good planted with *aurea,* a bright yellow-leaf berberis. I also have 'Red Glow', which is like *atropurpurea,* but the young leaves are mottled silver pink and bright rose.

Buddleia davidii
A favourite shrub for the butterflies, often called the 'Butterfly Bush'. One thing which is important with this plant is pruning; it should be cut back hard in March on last year's growth to within 2in of old wood, otherwise there will be a deficiency of flowers. I grow *Buddleia harlequin* which has strongly variegated cream leaves and purplish-red flowers.

Caryopteris
A delightful, small, blue-flowering shrub which took my eye years ago when I first saw it growing near Euonymus Silver Queen, the contrasting colours matching well. The *caryopteris* will take time to establish itself. In August, it will show clusters of small, fluffy, blue flowers. I have the variety 'Arthur Simmonds'.

Choisya (Mexican Orange Blossom)
Choisya ternata, as it is called, is a bright, good-looking evergreen shrub. The leaves are in triplets and bear bunches of white-scented, five-petalled blooms in May. The *choisya* which I am growing is a new variety from Blooms of Bressingham, called

Choisya 'Sundance'. The leaves are much more golden than the *ternata* and stand out well in a border. *Choisya* can't stand cold winds and frosts so a little protection is needed.

Cotinus rhus

The *Cotinus coggygria,* as it is now known (I wonder who thought of giving this delightful shrub such a mouthful of a name) has the bronze and purple colours of shrubs which I love. The *Cotinus* 'Royal Purple' which I grow lives up to its name as far as colour is concerned. The leaves colour well in the autumn, and if you prune hard in spring you will obtain some good, upright sprays forming a nice, bushy habit.

Daphne mezereum

No winter-flowering shrub is more colourful to start with new year than this one. It is a small shrub which rarely grows to more than 4ft high. Daphne's tiny, pink flowers are tubular, rather like little trumpets, growing in dense bunches up the stem, and are sweetly perfumed. This shrub was grown in cottage gardens by our forefathers, but it can be temperamental, especially if the soil becomes water-logged or there is a drought. The daphne bush does not take kindly to being moved and one must never be tempted to cut off sprays of the flowers to take indoors, as it will suffer and probably die. Just leave it to 'pride itself in the garden'.

Eleagnus pungens maculata

This shrub is commonly known as the Wild Olive and is, I think, one of the most striking shrubs we have. It can reach up to 12ft in height with leaves of tough, metallic sheen lavishly splashed with yellow; a most welcome sight in a winter garden. It is another useful shrub for the flower arranger. You don't have to worry about pruning; however, you will often get plain leaves instead of variegated, so just prune these pieces out. An easy-to-grow shrub for exposed sites.

Euonymus

There are two distinct groups – one which loses its leaves, and these are Spindleberries; the other, Radicans, I shall be writing about later. In my garden I grow 'Silver Queen' Variegata which is fairly slow growing with creamy-white and green leaves, and pretty, rose tints in winter. I also have 'Emerald 'n Gold', which is another outstanding foliage plant. These can be grown in poor soil and cuttings may be easily taken.

Hypericum (St John's Wort or Rose of Sharon)
Most people grow *hypericum* as ground cover since it flourishes under trees and on dry banks; but I grow *hypericum elstead,* a shrub growing to 4ft in height. Its flowers are small and bright red, and egg-shaped berries appear at the same time. I am very fond of this shrub; however, you will have to hunt for it in garden centres. One nurseryman told me that it suffers from rust but, 'touch wood', mine grows well in the border. The plant takes its country name from St John and is associated with the mystic rites of Midsummer's Eve, a celebration which goes back to pre-Christian days. The plant was also hung above the entrance to dwellings to prevent the entry of evil spirits.

Ilex (Holly)
The holly is the most accommodating of garden shrubs. 'Grow holly alongside your house as it is a protection against thunder and lightning' was one of the innumerable, old sayings about this popular shrub. The common holly is known by everyone for its deep-green leaves and bright-red berries. There are many varieties; remember that you will need male and female shrubs in order to obtain berries. An old gardener once told me that if a holly bush seeds itself in the garden it should never be disturbed as it will bring good luck to the owner. Pruning should be carried out in late June or July – hollies need at least some shortening to keep them in shape, but if it is necessary to cut back hard, this should be done in April on old holly and the task spread over two years or you could kill the shrub. I am pleased with the hollies in my garden as most were grown from cuttings. These are 'Silver Queen', (which by the way is male, variegated and has no berries) and 'Golden King', (which is female with large dark-green leaves splashed with golden

edges and has few berries). Another variety known as 'Golden Queen' is also perversely male! These hollies are somewhat of a joke because of their names – it's a rum old world, even in the garden, at times! Hollies will grow in most soils, need part sun and part shade and make excellent windbreaks.

Laurus (Bay Tree or Laurel)
The Romans loved to adorn the brows of their heroes with laurel and the French love the bay *Laurus Nobilus* for adding pungency to casserole dishes. I grow this variety in a tub so that I can put it in a cold greenhouse during the winter as it is susceptible to winter damage. *Laurus* may be planted in the garden, but choose a spot well sheltered from cold winds.

Osmanthus (Burkwoodii)
A fine evergreen with small oval-shaped, shiny leaves similar to holly.

White- or cream-coloured very fragrant flowers appear in April or May on growth made in the previous season. A hybrid cross between *delavayi* and what used to be called *Phillyrea decora*.

Philadelphus (Mock Orange or Orange Blossom)
The mock orange, as we know this shrub, will grow almost anywhere. I always think of weddings when I see this shrub in flower; its fragrance can be enjoyed at some distance away. I have often used it for decorating in church and the scent pervades the whole building. It is rather sad that the blooms last for only two to three weeks in June and all that remains is a shrub of little interest.

The *philadelphus* is a big family; I grow 'Enchantment', which is up to 7ft in height with small, white double flowers profusely borne on its arching branches. When these shrubs are pruned, immediately after flowering, cut out some of the old stems which have blossomed, making sure that the bush is not overcrowded.

Not the bridge over the River Kwai but over my small fish pool! With *hosta, mimulus* and *trollius (Clive Howard)*

A view from the kitchen window – looking towards *zephirine-drouhin rose*, mixed fuchsias and pots of lilies *(Clive Howard)*

Pittosporum tetuifolium
I had a super 10ft tree growing at one time, but the cold winter of a few years ago soon put paid to it. Most flower arrangers will know the value of a few pieces of pittosporum in their designs. It is one of my favourites, but it is very tender and I lose it in the winter. However, I am now growing one in a large pot, so hopefully I can keep it in a cold greenhouse throughout next winter! The attraction of pittosporum lies in its small, black twigs with tiny olive-green leaves. I have also seen 'Silver Queen' which has white splashes on the leaves.

Santolina (Cotton Lavender)
Cotton lavender is in no way related to the true lavender. I have seen it grown as a hedge plant just 2ft high with small, fleshy leaves covered in tiny, silvery hairs and small, round heads of yellow pompom flowers. In my garden I grow it as a shrub and gather the foliage occasionally as I love the pungent aroma. It is suited to most soils and may be planted in a sunny well-drained spot.

Senecio
A small shrub with yellow, daisy flowers; but it is the leaves which are rather special. A grey down seems to cover the foliage. I find the senecio needs to be cut back to keep it nice and compact. Sometimes the centre gets woody, so cut back and let it shoot from the bottom. Not all senecio are hardy, so choose a sheltered spot. For flower-arranging I stand them immediately in water, but not submerged as the leaves will turn greyish-black.

Spiraea
A popular group of shrubs with hordes of varieties, both spring and

Old wheelbarrows make useful containers – filled with fuchsias and lobelia *(Author)*

Old bottles and drain pipes make unusual containers – dripping with geraniums and fuchsias! *(Author)*

Autumn abundance

summer flowering. I suppose that most gardeners will know 'Bridal Wreath Arguta' which looks just like a bride's bouquet when in bloom with its masses of pure white blooms in the summer.

The *spiraea* take their name from the ancient Greek Speiraia, a plant used for garlands. I grow 'Anthony Waterer', a 2ft bush with flat heads of pink, crimson flowers, and 'Gold Flame' which has foliage of orange and yellow and looks good planted near blue 'Veronica'. The two above-named *spiraeas* need to be cut down each spring, 4–5in above ground level.

Syringa (Lilac)

I am lucky as I can see fields of lilac on my way into Woodbridge, which is the 'home' where these were first started. Notcutts Nurseries have a large collection as lilac is one of their specialities.

'Maud Notcutt' is a superb single white (the nicest white in this family) and lasts well when cut. I am only sorry that I am unable to grow these fine syringa as they are rather large shrubs and I simply do not have the room. I do grow, however, the super *Microphylla Superba* – the 'Little leaf lilac'. This is a slender, branched bush, pointed leaves and erect pinnacles of fragrant rosy pink flowers in May to June, then a bonus-blooming again in September. Flower-arrangers will love this shrub although it can reach up to 6ft in height. Little lilac has a delicious scent.

Viburnum

With the viburnums carefully planted you could have flowers all the year round; there are so many shapes and sizes and all sweetly perfumed. All are easy to grow and they do like plenty of good farmyard manure. I have *Bodnantense deben.* The blooms appear from October onwards and go on flowering all winter; white-pink tinted clusters growing on rather naked branches. This variety was raised at Notcutts Nurseries in Woodbridge, Suffolk. Do go to your local nursery and choose one or more for yourself.

Vibernum Tinus

This a good old stand-by for winter flower arrangements. A reliable evergreen, the flowers are in loose semi-snowballs, white turning pale pink. I am trying to grow the *variegatum* form, but this seems to be rather slow to get going.

Weigela

I think that the weigela is one of the easiest shrubs to grow, as the cuttings I take all seem to get established. They are deciduous and the little trumpet-like flowers of pink are very showy. Most soils will suit the weigela. One of the prettiest is the *Florida Variegata* which grows to 4–6ft and has rose-pink flowers in June and July. The compact, decorative foliage has green leaves with creamy-white edges. Her Royal Highness, Princess Margaret, remarked on the fact that this is a very pretty shrub when she visited my garden on a memorable summer day in 1984.

Climbers

Abutilon megapotanicum is a perfect climber in a sheltered position, or better still, grown in a cool greenhouse. I find this climber rather dainty, with its yellow bells and crimson calyxes. One must give the abutilon some form of support, because the plant has slender, lax and spreading stems and it will need to be grown upright to reveal the beauty of the flowers.

Actinidia kolomikta is an extraordinary climber with pale white and pink tips at the ends of the leaves. I think it was the fascination of the leaves which made me plant one in my garden. The variety I grow is not so vigorous as *chinensis* (which has egg-shaped fruits and is sold under the name of the Chinese Gooseberry Fruit Climber). I have the plant growing on a wooden fence facing south; the heart-shaped leaves keep throughout the season and the more the sun shines on them, the more variegated they become.

Clematis is such a big subject that I would recommend anyone specially interested to get in touch with a specialist grower. I am lucky as there is a specialist living only a few miles from my home – Fisks Clematis Nursery at Westleton, near Saxmundham, Suffolk. You can visit this nursery for friendly advice and the staff there will tell you which varieties will best suit your walls or fences.

The clematis is often called the 'queen of the climbers', but remember to have the 'head in the sun and feet in the cool' when planting. I put large stones on top of my soil when clematis has been planted, this helps to keep moisture in as well as preventing the sun drying out the roots. As there are many groups and families of this superb climber, I am just going to tell you the ones which I grow. The first on my list is *armandii* – this is a lovely evergreen clematis. It likes a warm wall and bears small, pale-pink flowers in the spring. I think that the green leathery leaves are as attractive as the bloom, but I must warn you that it can be cut down in very bad winters. Once it gets well established *armandii* will soon cover your fence. The *montana rubens* which I have growing over the garden arch and in the apple tree is an extremely hardy plant with small, deep rose-pink blooms and purple foliage. This clematis is happy growing in sun or shade, but it does require plenty of room. Another variety which I think should be grown more, is *tangutica*; an unusual and amazing climber and a rampant grower. It bears attractive, lantern-shaped, golden-yellow blooms from July to November and these are suspended from long wiry stems. The seed heads with their silver tassels are very effective for using in dry flower arrangements in the winter months. 'Nellie Moser' is another super plant with delicate, bluish-pink blooms having a deep carmine pink bar to each petal, which makes the whole flower stand out. My 'Nellie Moser' is planted over a garden arch next to the rose 'Canary Bird'. With the small, yellow flowers of the rose this makes a lovely contrast in colour. 'Madame-le-Coultre' has masses of large, pure white blooms with golden stamens and this I have planted near my wine shed.

Between my neighbour's garden and mine I have a wooden fence 48 yards long and the following clematis are planted along this fence to give colour through the summer. 'Dr Rupper', which is a rose colour with deep carmine bar and golden sepals, starts flowering in May and June, and again in September. Next to this I have 'Daniel Deronda' with violet blue and yellow stamens. The flowers are semi-double to start with, but by the end of the summer they are single. 'Niobe' is next, almost black in colour. This clematis has the most striking colour I have ever seen in this queen of climbers. The flowers appear in early June, continuing until September and are dark ruby, almost black pointed sepals with golden stamens. For a late-flowering variety I have 'Lady Betty Balfour'. This does need to be planted in full sun as the violet-blue flowers with yellow stamens need that little extra warmth. 'Twilight' is another pretty, deep mauve petunia-looking clematis; very free flowering, starting to flower in July and carrying on to October continuously. 'Mrs Choimondeley' has lavender-blue flowers with rather unusual brown stamens, flowering from May to October. This is a good grower.

One day your clematis may be fine, then suddenly the plant collapses – this is caused by the dreaded disease called wilt. Unfortunately, little is known about this fungus. Some horticulturists will say that it is in the soil previous to the attack and a damaged stem will pick up the fungus. Don't give up, all is not lost. If you think that the plant has wilt, the roots should still be in good form. Cut the plant right down, burn the affected parts and spray around the roots with Benlate; this is a good systemic fungicide. Make a point of giving the rest of your clematis a spray every two weeks with Benlate; prevention is better than cure.

Ceanothus or Californian lilac is a native of California and likes a warm spot, but I have been surprised how some tolerate the cold winds and hard frosts. I once had *Ceanothus veitchianus* growing on my wine shed, but the cold hard winter of 1984 killed it. I don't like to be without these most attractive blue-flowering shrubs and I have planted another *Burkwoodii* near the wall of my house. Some forms are more hardy than others. 'Delight' is another hardy; but all varieties like a warm, south- or west-facing wall.

Fremontia californica is a wall shrub which was seldom seen at one time, but over the last few years I have seen some fine specimens. It is semi-evergreen and will thrive in the most sun-drenched soil, even poor soil. The flowers are richly coloured yellow and are quite spectacular. It is best planted near a wall to show off the beauty of the flowers and you will find that it can reach up to 20ft in height.

Garrya elliptica, or silk tassel bush, is a most delightful plant for a fence or wall, and much more popular now than it was a few years ago. I have a feeling that this is what flower arrangers have done for us, as demonstrators of the art like to use this shrub in early winter. The garrya is best known for its long and slender catkins. There are male and female forms and, dare I say it, the male form is the most elegant. When cut for decoration the catkins last a long time. The plant is hardy and should be grown in loamy soil.

Hedera or ivy. The common ivy tends to become a troublesome plant and many would say, why grow ivy in the garden? I can assure you that the new ivies which are in today's catalogues are fascinating to grow. They range from the small-leaved, one inch across to larger specimens which are five inches across or more and either plain or variegated. I have a 'Goldheart' growing on my toolshed with an annual climber called *Eccremocapus scaber,* with its red flowers, intertwining amongst the 'Goldheart'; it presents quite a contrast of colour. The other form which I have is *Denata variegata;* with its yellow-edged leaves it makes a good cover for any fence or shed.

Hydrangea petiolaris or Japanese climbing hydrangea. Once you get this plant going it can be a vigorous climber; but I find that it will take a year or two to get established before really starting to grow. I can't really understand why more people don't grow this hardy climber, as it is suitable for walls of any aspect. The hydrangea will soon cover the wall or fence, but you may have to provide some form of support during the early stages of its growth. The glossy leaves are broad and deep green and the clusters of flat, creamy-white flowers 6–8in across are a sight to behold in early summer.

Lonicera The common name of this plant is honeysuckle, and it must be one of our oldest climbers. The scent is wonderful in the early mornings and late evenings. Living in the country with the blackbird's song and the smell of honeysuckle – and all for free – is a wonderful gift. I can understand why, years ago, the 'little house' (bumby) down the bottom of the cottage garden, had honeysuckle growing all over it!!

The varieties are numerous. The one I have is sometimes called Japanese honeysuckle, mainly because of its yellow, mottled leaves; the white flowers are much smaller than those of the larger varieties. *Aureoreticulata* is grown over an archway with the annual *Cobaea scandens* (Cup and Saucer Plant) which has purple flowers. I also grow the early and late forms 'Belgica' and 'Serotina' to spread blooms from May to October. The woodbine honeysuckle, as it was called, was the ancient symbol of fidelity and true love.

Pyracantha or Fire Thorns, has brilliant orange, scarlet and yellow berries in autumn and winter. I have *angusifolia* growing on the side of the house. The leaves are narrow and the orange-yellow, berries remain on this pyracantha longer than on my other variety called 'Mohave', which has red berries all along the branches. This much improved form and the *angustifolia* pyracantha are from the rose family. A well-trained 'Mohave' against the wall gives brilliant winter colour with its evergreen, glossy foliage and huge trusses of red berries. Some people say that the birds won't touch the berries unless the winter is severe, but don't you believe it. My berries are often all gone well before the snow and hard frosts arrive.

Solanum jasminoides A member of the potato family, with its spectacular show of bluish-purple flowers hanging in clusters with yellow anthers; a very pretty sight in the summer months. I grow *solanum crispum* which can reach heights of up to 20ft. I would not say that it is hardy as I have lost two of my plants in the past few years, but I do take cuttings in August. It is a climber well worth having, but sadly it is not grown very much these days in cottage gardens.

Some Favourite Roses

American Pillar

This is an old rose which has a crimson, rambler-type growth. If you grow it you will see that the best blooms are borne on the one-year-old shoots. This means pruning and cutting out annually a few of the oldest growths. American Pillar is a vigorous rose with strong thorny stems and glossy leaves. The single, red flowers soon turn to a pale pink and their large trusses are a picture to be seen on my fence in the summer. There is, however, one fault I find with this rose; it has no resistance to mildew.

Dorothy Perkins, better known as Excelsa

My grandfather used to have this rampant grower near the 'little house' down the garden. This pretty, rambler rose will grow in

Universal favourites

most areas of the garden, all it will need is support. The colourful cascades of clear, pink flowers appear in July. It is another rose which is susceptable to mildew, so try and keep it away from other roses – it looks very good on a fence or archway.

Handel

This is the rose for me! The unique colouring of the blooms is so pretty, even the dark green, almost purple leaves are good for rose foliage. I like the way the large semi-double flowers open to whitish-pink with red marking on the edges of the petals. Flowers appear either in clusters or singly. I think that this makes a good climber trained against a wall, and must be one of the most successful and popular of roses to come out of the specialist nurseries during the last twenty years.

New Dawn

Another good rose, especially if you need to cover a wall or fence quickly. For over forty years this silvery-pink rose has been very popular. Flowering early, around June, it also carries blooms into late summer. The buds are charmingly long, pointed and firm, but open too quickly into somewhat loosely formed flowers. The blooms may be cut for flora work as the flowers are borne on long stems. An ideal rambling rose.

Parkdirektor Riggers

This must be one of the best red climbers. The large clusters of glowing, crimson blooms are on nice long stems which start to flower in June and, if dead-heading is kept up, continuous flowering will result. I leave the blooms on my climbers at the end of September to produce some lovely red hips which will stay on the bush until Christmas, and I then use them for decorating our church for the festive season. A good spraying for mildew and blackspot should be religiously carried out during the summer months.

School Girl .

There are not many orange climbing roses, so I suppose the colour took my eye when I bought this one. The orange blooms are large, fragrant and borne singly – sometimes there may be a small mass of flowers, but not very often. A vigorous climber and disease resistant.

Shot Silk

I think this must be the oldest rose I have in my garden, planted over the front door. Always the first to bloom, round about late May, its flowers are of a pink, silky texture with a golden-yellow centre. 'Shot Silk' has a nice coppery, glossy foliage; also a heavenly scent. I always think that after the first blooms the next display is rather disappointing.

Zephirine Drouhin
Every gardener should plant this rose if he has the space. It is excellent for continuity of flowering. After over a hundred years this thornless rose has a rich perfume and is still a strong grower. The flowers are semi-double cerise pink. A great favourite of mine.

As well as climbers, here are a few shrub roses:–

Canary Bird
You will need plenty of room for this rose. The foliage is very pretty, fern-like, on long arching shoots. From May onwards 'Canary Bird' produces bright yellow, single flowers which last for about four weeks. I like the graceful habit of this shrub, and a standard form also looks good. It will also be popular with flower arrangers.

Cecile Brunner or Sweetheart Rose
Once you have this plant you will understand why it is called the Sweetheart Rose. Many times I have been asked if I can spare a few buds for putting in a vase on top of a wedding cake. Nothing can replace the charm of the tiny, pink flowers at the bud stage. They form in clusters, but Cecile Brunner is not a very robust grower (3–4ft) and sometimes takes three years to reach full stature. Do not over-do the pruning.

Perle d'Or
This is another small rose, remarkably similar to 'Cecile Brunner'. Only the colour is different – instead of pink blooms, 'Perle d'Or' has clusters of creamy-buff flowers, slightly perfumed.

Rose de L'Hay
Undoubtedly one of the finest of the Rugosas, if you have the room to grow it. In my garden the size has reached over 6ft high and 8ft wide. I like this rose for the petals, used in making rose petal wine. You don't get any disease on the bright-green foliage and a double bonus is that the leaves turn a nice orange-brown colour in autumn. The individual, purple flowers do not last long, but there always seem to be more blooms coming along.

Rosa moyesii

A fine specimen of a shrub rose, there are several varieties of the *moyesii.* The one I grow is named 'Geranium', less vigorous than the parent. The flowers come in late May and June, sometimes carrying on until late July, and are brilliant crimson-red single blooms. Even the centre of the bloom is creamy, which sets off the flower to perfection. But I must confess that I like the rose best for its fruits. In the autumn come the most striking bottle-shaped hips, glossy red 2–2½in long.

Rosa Mundi

This is one of the oldest of the Gallica roses and 'Mundi' appears to date back to 1581. But whatever the age, I find it one of the most enchanting, with distinctly striped flowers in pink and white. The bush only grows to about 4ft high, but look out for suckers, which come freely.

And last but not least:

Rosa Rubrifolia

This again is a special rose for the flower arranger; a wild rose from central Europe, grown for its foliage. The small, purplish-pink flowers appear in June. They are not showy blooms, in fact, quite insignificant, but I love the leaves of purplish-brown colour. Even the stems are a reddish brown and almost thornless. Some of my rubrifolias grow to 8ft or more, but they can be pruned to a size to fit any garden. In the autumn, some nice hips will appear.

Pot Pourri

Many of the herbs and plants may be used for making pot pourris to have in bowls about the house. At one time pot pourri bowls were to be found in almost every home, but now they are confined mostly to country cottages and manor houses. The bowls, of decorated china or wood, usually have lids pierced with holes in the top, thus allowing the perfume to escape whilst at the same time keeping the 'mixture' free from dust. A pot pourri can give much pleasure but its appeal will depend on the mixture used to make the scent. Dried petals of honeysuckle, dried herbs like marjoram, rosemary and thyme and even the skin of dried orange, plus a pinch or two of crushed cloves may be mixed. But, as with all perfumes, one which may be acceptable to a person who enjoys a sweet perfume may be unacceptable to one who would like a more refreshing fragrance.

To make a moist pot pourri, which will be even more powerfully fragrant, begin by placing a 6in layer of rose petals, undried, into an earthenware jar, cover with a thin layer of salt and allow to settle. Then, as the season advances, add the petals of pinks, orange blossom and more rose petals, each time covering with a layer of salt and keeping the jar quite closed. Finally, some dried orange skin, mixed with a good pinch of dried cloves and dried marjoram. Keep closed until the perfume is to be enjoyed.

Scented geranium are especially suited to making pot pourri. The plants were used years ago for sweetening the musty, damp rooms of cottages, the leaves being very fragrant (not the flowers). Victorians would plant the scented geraniums near the edge of garden borders, where the brushing of the leaves with the long period clothes would create the most lovely fragrance.

Varieties of scented geraniums are pelargonium *capitatum*, p. *crispum variegatum*, p. *crispum* 'Minor', p. *crispum* 'Major'–richly lemon scented, and p. *tomentosum*.

This is the same plant used by Gertrude Jekyll to make peppermint jelly, and used to be found often in old-fashioned gardens.

Nowadays the lady of the house has push button sprays to use, but years ago in Edwardian times maids used to first burn cypress wood to clear rooms of any bad smells, then they would put together a small pinch of sugar and rose water, boil the mixture and pour over the hot cypress wood embers. It is said that the room would be filled with a smell of roses. Another old perfume was made by powdered cloves mixed with rose water and boiled. I bet there was a good smell from that pan!

Rose petals are most in demand for making pot pourri, but it is often said that the petals are not picked at the right stage. All too often the flowers are allowed to be past their best before being used.

If a member of your household is unwell, why not make up a rose petal bag to hang on the bedrail. Gather rosebuds just as they are about to open, dry them in an airy room, then take some powdered cinnamon or cloves and add dried leaves of marjoram, orange blossom or any other sweet-smelling flower which has been dried. Make a little bag and put all flowers inside, tieing it with a ribbon bow – a charming gift.

It is not an easy job to dry rose petals. They should be collected when quite dry and after the early morning dew has disappeared. Just take a few heads off at a time; you can't hurry a pot pourri. My petals are placed on wire lined cake-trays and dried in my spare bedroom. This, I find, is a good, cool place in summer, away from the rays of the sun. Turn them regularly so that they dry quickly, otherwise mildew may soon appear. Once the petals are dry, pack them into a glass jar, making sure that it has a good seal – you don't want all your time and effort wasted if they turn mouldy through letting moisture into the container.

⋙⋙ The Greenhouse ⋘⋘

All keen gardeners will need a greenhouse. The first thing to think about is the size you will need. Believe me, you will never get one big enough. I have two, one 19ft x 8ft and the other 10ft x 8ft, and still I don't have enough room come spring!! So be guided and try to buy the biggest one that will fit into your garden. The next main job is to choose a situation which will give maximum sunlight and yet is sheltered from north and north-east winds. The greenhouse should normally be sited north to south to ensure the maximum average sunlight and reduce the shading to a minimum during the course of the year, (it is estimated that in winter the light loss due to dirty glass and doors can be as high as 50 per cent). I would like at this point to provide a few tips about your site and erection of the greenhouse:

1 Do try to choose a sunny site and never place a greenhouse under a tree.
2 Think about heating. If you are going to use electricity, try to place your greenhouse as close to the house as possible, as electric wiring can be costly.
3 Don't put your greenhouse near the road or the play-area.

Now, choosing between wood or aluminium. I am lucky as I have one of each. My wooden one is very good, made of red cedar, and looks attractive. It does, however, need to have a wood preservative each year if you can find the time. Also after a few years the wood starts to rot if it is not looked after. Aluminium is more popular and easier to maintain, but I find the wooden one is the warmer of the two. There is also a polythene construction, but it has a limited life, (if you do choose plastic, it should be UV Stabilised).

Once the greenhouse is erected, do think about ventilators.

Although the greenhouse has windows there are times when you have to go out and the temperature will get up to 80°F or 90°F. If you have automated ventilators you won't regret it. They start to open the window when the temperature reaches 70°F, so you won't find the plants burnt-up on your return. I have louvred side ventilators which are very good, but make sure when they are closed that they are properly closed or you will soon get a draught.

You will also need staging. Try to get one to fit the back wall, but it's no good getting one which is too low. You can make your own, or there is a collapsible one available on the market today which can be taken down in the summer months to enable you to grow tomatoes or tall flowering plants etc.

A most essential extra is a power point fixed in the greenhouse; but remember, this needs to be regularly checked for working order. You will need this for your propagator, already indicated as a must for any greenhouse, and also, of course, your light fixture. Heating the greenhouse can prove very expensive. Electricity is the most popular method. Apart from the running costs, it has every advantage. Electricity can be thermostatically controlled and I find that it needs the minimum of attention, although we do run the risk of power-cuts. My heater is of the tubular type, running around the sides of both houses and providing heat which is evenly spread in each of them. I also line the greenhouses with bubble plastic in winter months to help keep warmth in. Most amateurs will go for paraffin heaters which are cheap to buy and to run; but there can be problems, like water vapour, which increases the risk of disease. A blue-flame model must be obtained and the wick trimmed regularly. A friend of mine used a paraffin heater in the greenhouse and one night the wick was left rather high; the flame got up and the whole greenhouse was black with thick smoke next morning, and all the plants inside were lost. But I must say that if paraffin heaters are looked after carefully they can be a useful stand-by to keep the chill off a small house, or during a power failure. The other types of heating are natural gas or bottled gas. These are both good, but as with the paraffin heater, water vapour can be a problem. I expect you will say that I use the most expensive form of heating, but gardening is my hobby and as long as I can keep my stock of plants through the winter, I don't mind. I only keep the temperature at 38–40°F. There is a traditional type of greenhouse heater – the solid fuel-fired boiler – but they are not used as much nowadays. They need regular stoking and cleaning, but do provide a good alternative to electricity or paraffin. Gas is another form of heater, using natural gas; it is compact, automatic in operation and simple to install. Accurate thermostatic control makes it a cheap fuel, but of course, this means you must have gas nearby. We in the country don't have a supply of gas, only the bottled sort.

Next on the list would be to buy a thermometer, a maximum/minimum is best which you can see at eye-level. If you place it on the north side it will tell you how the temperature drops at night, if you set it for this information. Remember that plants are harmed by widely-fluctuating temperatures.

Hygiene is very important to any gardener; remember 'cleanliness is next to godliness', if pests and diseases are to be kept at bay. I use a lot of Jeyes Fluid around my garden and in the greenhouses, sterilising the base, seed trays and pots and wiping regularly with diluted household bleach as well.

Another item you should try to get is a cold frame. These are used for hardening off plants that have just come out of the greenhouse, for striking cuttings and also for growing melons and cucumbers; in fact they have many uses.

Pot Plants

My hints for house plants are from my own experience! It is not easy to define a house plant as there are quite a large number of plants which are suitable. Some can be grown indoors for a long time, whilst others will only survive for a few weeks.

One of the most important factors for success with house plants is light. (Of all the questions I am asked on my radio programme, those concerning house plant problems are the most frequent; queries like 'Why are the leaves turning yellow?', or 'Why are there no flowers?', to quote but two.) People tend to buy plants on sight, take them home, stick them on top of the television set or in the front window and leave them to it. This shows no feeling for the poor old plant. Another thing I hate to see are plants which have been standing in the market in rough winds and cold weather. Is there any wonder, taking the plant into a warm room, that the leaves suddenly drop or the flower buds fall off? If you want a good house plant, buy it at a reliable nursery. Now, getting back to light – some plants won't even flower if they don't get light; some will flourish on a sunny window sill but quickly deteriorate in a shady corner, while others will grow in light shade but cannot survive exposure to sunlight. Here are some danger signs to look for, if your plant is not getting enough light: spindly growth or no growth at all, variegated leaves turning green, poor blooms or none at all, bottom leaves falling or turning yellow. If you have too much light the plants will get scorch patches on their leaves and lower leaves will soon wilt, at about midday.

Next you need to know when to feed – plants are like us humans, they need nourishment. When first bought the plant will have sufficient food in the pot for a time. Plants in their full growth require liquid manure while plants in their resting period should not be fed. Most growing plants can be fed once or twice a week with liquid manure. I find it best to give them a weak solution of liquid manure once a week rather than a strong solution every other week. 'How much liquid feed?' you ask. I give a dessertspoonful of liquid manure in about 4 pints of water to about 16–20 plants. There are many brands of plant food on the market, (I have cow manure in a sack in an old water tank, so I am lucky as I always have my liquid feed on hand). Another tip to remember is that plants do like to have resting periods, when they require less water and feeding. I will explain this when I talk about each pot plant.

Potting can be confusing to some people and they tend to re-pot plants which have not flowered. If this is done, it will only give the roots more room to make more growth, hence no flowers. The tighter the roots are, the more likelihood of flowers. When re-potting, try to use the same kind of potting soil as that in which the plant is already growing. Gone are the days when we used to wait for a horse to go by, and then collect the droppings. When the mole left a neat pile of soil in the meadow, my father used to ask me to collect some in a bucket. But, of course, there was no good soil compost to buy in those days, and farm workers would not dream of buying soil. My father would have a fit if he could see the amount of compost that I buy each year. A typical loam-based compost consists of seven parts, measured by bulk, of sterilised loam, three parts granulated peat, one part sharp sand, with fertiliser added to provide nitrogen, phosphate and potassium. All plants need a free-draining compost. Azaleas, heathers, camellias, cyclamen, fern and a number of plants which come from the tropical rain forests, need a peat-based compost. When you do re-pot make sure that you have good drainage at the bottom of the pot. If you can't find a few pieces of broken clay pot, put a piece of foam at the bottom before adding your compost. Leave space ¾–1 in from the top of the pot so there is room for watering. Daily spraying of the leaves will help the plant to recover more quickly from the shock of re-potting. Don't start to feed for about three weeks.

Thinking about pot plants takes me back to my childhood when I used to grow plants from pips and tops cut from vegetables. Next time you eat an orange or grapefruit, try saving the seeds or pips.

You won't get fruit true to the seed but you can get nice, interesting little trees. For citrus fruit, save the pips from really ripe fruit. Put five pips in a 4in pot and plant them on their sides about ½in below the compost and water carefully. They take about 3–4 weeks to shoot. Move each pip on to its own 4in pot when it has a pair of leaves, and stand it outside for the summer. (Don't let them dry out!) Move to a bigger pot each year and enjoy your tree. I am often asked about avocado stones; these do make nice pot plants and will grow into really big bushes. You start them off in water; get four cocktail sticks and stick them into the stone about three-quarters of the way down. Suspend the stone over a jar of water, keeping the end of the stone in the water. Roots will grow in about three to four weeks. When you have several roots put up in compost, leaving the top half of the stone sticking out of the compost. When you have a shoot out of the top, let it grow to about 6–8in tall, then cut the top off so that you get a bushy plant (so many people let them grow and they get too lanky). Nip out the tips of new side shoots when they get 6in long as this will encourage more side branches to form. You can also grow plants from date stones, but don't expect a big date tree! The stones should be soaked for 2–3 days in warm water, then put in a bag of moist peat. Keep them in a warm place until you see roots appear, then plant each stone in compost, one to each pot. They will grow slowly at first but after one year will start to look like a small palm bush. Water well in summer but not too much in winter. Carrots and beetroot will make pretty leaves if you cut off the tops about ½in from the top and stand in a dish of water on the kitchen window-sill.

Here is a handy hint for those who are going on holiday, and are worried about leaving their house plants. Put all the plants in the sink and stand a bucket of water on the draining board. Take lengths of thick knitting wool, putting one end of the wool in the bucket and the other to the pot plant, (large plants may need two lengths of wool), and this will create a capillary action. Of course, if you have a lot of plants you can always stand them in the bath (put an old bath mat in first so as not to scratch the surface) with a bucket on a stool standing in the middle of the bath, and with plants surrounding the stool.

Some varieties of pot plants are as follows:

Aspidistra (Cast Iron Plant)
This was seen in all cottage windows years ago (behind a net curtain). It was the Victorians favourite plant, and the only feed it used to get was cold tea. It gets its nick-name from the fact that it was able to withstand neglect. It is one of the flower arrangers dreams as the leaves dry very well. Of recent years some plants have been very expensive, making £1.00 per leaf. The variegated plant is much sought after nowadays. Aspidistras do flower, but the bloom is very small and is produced at ground level; so you might even miss seeing it flower. Divide in spring but do not re-pot too frequently as they are slow growers. I find that they can be sensitive to chemicals and insecticides. They thrive in almost all living room conditions and can withstand considerable extremes of light and heat; but keep out of strong sunlight as this may scorch the leaves. Brown marks on the leaves are often a sign of over-watering.

Begonia
There are so many species and hybrids of begonia, I will just give you one or two varieties. Fibrous rooted begonias are grown both for their flowers and decorative foliage. The flowers vary in size and colour but most have only single flowers. Rhizomatous begonias are primarily grown for their foliage. The most popular are the tuberous begonias which bloom in summer and autumn. All can be raised by planting tubers in February and March. Put the tubers in boxes of moist peat in a warm place. When shoots are a couple of inches high, pot up into 5in pots, moving on to larger pots as they grow. When the flowering season is over, lift corms if planted outside, and turn pots on their sides to dry, withholding water. Dry the tubers in peat away from frosts. Use coarse leaf mould or a peat-based mixture for potting up. Tubers can be cut into two or four when they are large, but treat with a sulphur dust to prevent Botrytis.

Chlorophytum eomosum 'Variegatum' (Spider Plant)
This is a very common plant. I think anyone can grow this as it is

so tough and adaptable. The most common fault is that it often gets brown tips on its leaves. This can be due to a lot of dry air and the fact that so often people forget to feed it. You will know when this plant needs re-potting because a mass of fleshy roots will start to lift the plant out of the pot. Compost on open soil mixture is best. Propagate by taking small plants off the parent plant.

Cissus Antarctica (Kangaroo Vine)
One of the most useful climbers to have for the home; it's a rampant grower. This plant is particularly good in a shady room but is often lost due to over-watering. Use a soil-based compost. Move plants into pots one size larger each spring. If plant is fed it can reach a height of 6ft. Once maximum size is reached, top dress with fresh compost each spring.

Coleus labitae (Flame Nettle)
These plants are grown for their foliage. They are difficult to overwinter but are easy to take from cuttings. Once you have got a plant going, do pinch out all the growing points several times a year – this helps them to stay bushy. They like a liquid feed every two weeks throughout the active growth period. Try not to let them dry out as you will soon get leaf drop. Use a soil-based potting mixture. *Coleus* like a bright light is possible. Insufficient light will result in spindly, elongated growth.

Cyclamen Primulaceae
If I had to choose just twelve house plants, the cyclamen would be one of them. I get more questions about cyclamen on my radio programmes than about any other plant. Where so many people go wrong with cyclamen is in over-watering and keeping them in a room which is too hot. Often they have to suffer such drastic changes of conditions between the flower shop and the home. Cyclamen should be given bright light without direct sunlight – a north-facing windowsill is ideal.

In spite of what other people say, I still like to water most of my plants from the bottom of the pot, but with the cyclamen you will soon rot the tuber if you take no precautionary measures. I stand my plants in dishes of small stones which I can keep damp. Remove faded flowers or yellowing leaves by a sharp pull of the stem, so that the stem comes cleanly from the corm or tuber, and don't leave short stumps to rot. Once the plant has finished flowering you can stand it outside, reducing watering to rest it until August when it can be started into growth once more. A peat-based compost is satisfactory. Feed every two weeks when new growth appears after dormancy. You can get very nice cyclamen from seeds sown in autumn, but they will take about eighteen months to flower.

Euphorbia pulcherrima (Poinsettia)

I love the story about the poinsettia, one of my favourite pot plants. It was Christmas Eve in Mexico and the music was merry. A poor, little girl named Maria was very sad as she watched all the villagers pass her on their way to church with presents for the Baby Jesus. She had no money and no present to give. She ran into a house and picked up a cup, thinking that it was beautiful. Running along she dropped the cup, breaking it in small pieces. This made her more sad as she now had nothing to give. As she sat by the roadside, she noticed a small plant. 'I will give this' she thought, for even the humblest offering given with love, is beautiful in His sight. She ran to the church and laid her gift on the altar saying 'With all my love'. As she left, the lights seemed to become brighter and brighter and her plant began to turn bright red. Others knelt in amazement at this wonderful change of the simplest offering, which has become known as 'The flower of the Nativity'.

Exacum affine (Persian Violet)

This is a small plant which grows to between 9 and 12in tall and is easy to grow from seed. It is naturally bushy and the small, fragrant flowers are abundant. Their colour is lavender blue, just like violets. They flower five months from sowing and I find that they last very well in the summer. 'Midget' is a good variety to grow. One thing to remember: never let *Exacum* dry out otherwise the flowers will shrivel up and die; also make sure that you take fading blooms off the plant, ensuring continuity of flowers.

Fatsia aralia (Castor Oil Plant)
I love this plant, especially *Fatsia japonica variegata.* They make fine specimens for living rooms, or for containers on a patio outside. These plants don't like too much heat. I have the green-leaved variety planted in the open garden. Try and find a sheltered spot and plant-out about mid-April so that it can settle in before the coming winter. If it is in the house, poor light will make your plant thin and pale, and too much heat will turn the leaves yellow. During the active growth period give plenty of water, keeping the compost moist, but in the winter months allow the top inch of soil to dry out (but not too much as the bottom leaves will fall off). Give a feed every ten days. I also find with the *Fatsia* that you need to plant in heavy clay pots as the plants get top heavy in plastic containers.

Ferns
There are many varieties, in fact over a thousand for indoor planting alone. I will give you some facts about the ones which I have come to love and enjoy over the years, and the varieties which are most popular today. Years ago, in Victorian times, most people had a fern in the front parlour.

I expect a lot of people will think that asparagus *sprengeri* and *plumosus* are the most popular of ferns. In fact, they are not ferns at all but foliage plants which are grown for their attractive, feathery foliage, which is why they have fern names. *Plumosus* is a fine plant used frequently by florists. I have one growing in the middle of the greenhouse making an archway with a 12ft spread. It often has red berries in the autumn and also some sharp prickles on the lower stems. I find this plant most useful when making up a bouquet or flower arrangement. The plant needs a light place, and a weekly dose of liquid manure keeps it looking green. If you have one in the house, syringing it with water is beneficial during the winter months, especially in a heated room.

The *sprengeri* variety is also a good foliage plant; its leaves are not so fine as the *plumosus,* but the florists use this in arrangements too. It is often sold for use in a hanging basket. As a house plant it is one of the easiest to grow. Again this plant only needs a slightly heated room and the leaves often drop off in the winter if the plant is allowed to dry out.

Asplenium nidus (Birds Nest Fern) Over the years this has become a popular house plant. I like the glossy, bright green leaves. It is said that it resembles a birds nest. Since *asplenium* (nidus) comes from the tropical forests it will need a heated room. You will soon notice if the plant is not getting enough warmth as the new leaves will acquire brown spots and the edges of the leaves will turn a rusty-brown. The fronds (leaves) may grow 3–4ft long. It is fascinating to see how it grows as the new fronds unroll from the central fibrous core. The plant likes plenty of water in season, but is best kept only moist in winter. I also like to feed every ten days with liquid manure.

Adiantum (Maidenhair Fern) This is a delicate and attractive little fern, one of my favourites with its triangular, light green fronds. This plant has seeded itself into the crevices of my damp greenhouse where it has flourished for years without any soil. It likes a shady position, but if you grow it indoors and have heated rooms, you should stand the pot on a tray of pebbles and mist-spray daily. The plant should only be slightly moist at the roots.

Platycerium (Stags Horn Fern) This fern can be cultivated in many ways. Its home is in the tropical forests, growing high up in the trees. It gets its name because it grows into a shape like stag's antlers. The fern does well when grown on pieces of rough bark. I find it best to grow this fern in a hanging basket fixed to a piece of bark. The stags horn does not like strong sunlight but it does like warmth. Try and spray once a day with a mist-spray and don't let the temperature drop below 60°F.

When bought, ferns are often growing on a piece of bark. Once it has outgrown this, fasten the fern onto a larger piece of bark by tying two pieces together with some sphagnum moss, making sure to keep the moss damp at the roots. Give a feed to mature plants every four weeks or so by immersing the basket for a few minutes. (I use an old baby's bath). After the bubbles cease to rise, it is time to take the plant out. Stand on the draining board to drain, then hang up.

Ficus

When we talk about *ficus,* most people will say 'Oh yes, a rubber tree', but there are all sorts of *ficus;* in fact, over 800 species of hardy and tender shrubs, including the ornamental rubber tree and weeping fig. I get a lot of questions about the rubber tree, *Ficus elastica.* The biggest challenge with this plant is not to lose the lower leaves. I feel that one of the most common faults is over-watering in winter with a sudden drop in temperature.

The *Ficus elastica* is the most popular of all the *ficus,* having large, shiny, leathery leaves. I like to see the bright red sheath which covers the new leaves, it just drops off as new leaves uncurl. If the sheath is pale in colour, it is not getting proper light. This plant can reach a height of over 12ft; to make the plant branch out you have to cut the growing point. There will be sap, like a bleeding, but you can remedy this by applying dry Benlate Powder (I have even used coal dust and green sulphur), it just needs something to stop the flow of sap. Cuttings can be obtained by taking the tip of the plant, about 6–8in long, in the spring. Insert in a 4in pot – I use equal parts of damp peat, sharp sand and perlite. I use a lot of perlite as I feel that this helps to let air into the compost. Your cuttings should take about 12–14 weeks to root. As the *Ficus elastica* has shiny leaves, it will need to have its leaves sponged regularly to keep the dust from accumulating. I should add this point – do be careful not to scratch the leaves or let the cat get to the plant, as the leaves will never recover and will remain scarred for their lifetime. Give actively growing plants a feed every two weeks. It likes a temperature of 55°F–60°F between winter and spring.

The *Ficus benjamina,* or weeping fig, is a more graceful and smaller leaved plant. I think it is very pretty; the leaves are a bright, light green, but as the plant gets older they turn to a much darker green.

Ficus pumila or creeping fig has a creeping habit, hence the name. It has heart-shaped leaves and produces aerial roots. I like to see this plant growing on a moss pole, but most people use it as a trailing plant. The creeping fig will tolerate more shade than other varieties of the *ficus* family. It likes a humid atmosphere so it would benefit from a daily spray using tepid water; with such care you should be able to enjoy this plant for many years. Sometimes you will come across the variegated form in shops; this will need more light than the plain green variety.

Fuchsia

This must be one of my top ten pot plants. The first fuchsia was introduced to Great Britain in 1788 by a Captain Firth. Most gardeners will know what an enormous number of fuchsias there are.

I feel lucky to be in East Anglia with Ipswich as my home town, for it has one of the biggest and most flourishing fuchsia societies, belonging to the British Fuchsia Society. A great number of the visitors to my garden during the year are enthusiasts and conversation is often about fuchsias.

Although these plants can be grown quite easily from seed, I find it more satisfactory to grow cuttings from named varieties, and one can soon swap cuttings with friends. They grow more profusely and stronger outside than under glass, but they like to be protected from the hot midday sun. I like to grow my plants in pots then plant outside. I do have hardy fuchsias but find that they don't start to flower until the end of July. Fortunately I have a selection of old sinks and drain-pipes which I use for my plants and this gives me varying heights. Fuchsias are adaptable plants and can be easily trained to all kinds of shapes. Visitors to the garden are amazed at our hanging baskets, which are full of flower in July, and even more amazed when I tell them that 'it's cuttings from early spring that do the trick'.

Basket fuchsias should have a pendulous habit and I like to start making up my baskets and containers in late February or early March, making sure that each basket is strong enough to take the weight of its contents! A large container can weigh as much as twelve pounds or more when in full flower. Be sure to check your chains. I once lost a lovely hanging basket full of the variety 'Campanella', when the chains snapped. When planting up your basket, allow three to four plants for a 12in size. I stand my basket on top of a bucket; it's easy to plant if the container sits nicely and doesn't wobble about.

When you start to grow fuchsias, you will find that they will soon 'grow on you'! You will get to know the varieties which you like, those which are strong growers and the ones which suit your containers; whether they are for a hanging basket, a window box or exhibits for the local flower show. It is very satisfying to start by growing your own cuttings. There is no set rule, but I will tell you how I take mine – it will be a guideline to follow.

A cutting is part of a live plant. There are many types, but I am only concerned here with the tip, which should be about 1½in in length with no flower buds and two or three pairs of leaves. Cut just below a leaf joint or node with a sharp razor-blade. I then dust the trimmed base with hormone rooting powder before placing it in a 2in pot of peat, sand and perlite (don't forget to put a label inside the pot). Give the cutting a watering, then place in a propagator and you should have rooted cuttings in about four weeks. After about six to seven weeks you will have to move your cuttings into a larger 4in pot. It will then be up to you to decide what sort of plant you wish to grow. If you want to make a bush, just pinch out the main growing shoot of the stem, then after three pairs of leaves have formed it will be time to start shaping the plant. Nip out the growing tip as this will encourage the production of side shoots, which in their turn should be nipped out after each has two pairs of leaves continuing until you have a nice round bush. The plant should also be moved to a larger pot each time the root ball fills up, so that the plant will keep steadily growing. Another point to remember is to turn your plant every two days or so, to help maintain balanced growth.

Once you have the fuchsia 'bug' you may wish to grow for exhibition. Show plants have to be trained and the required shape determines how many pinches are made; this can mean six, or even seven, stops before near perfection is achieved. After each stop flowering is delayed by eight to thirteen weeks, but the 'Triphyllas' and 'Species' types of fuchsia are all different. With a little bit of luck you should end up having a superb well-branched plant.

To make a standard fuchsia you must choose a good, strong grower. It is not as difficult as many people think. The cutting is struck in the normal manner as for a bush, but the main stem is allowed to grow on, instead of being nipped out. All the side shoots are removed as they grow but the main leaves are left until the required height is attained and the head is beginning to take shape. Don't forget to put a cane against the whip (this is what we call a standard cutting). To get a straight stem it is essential to tie your whip to a cane. Ties should be placed about 4in apart. Do check regularly, making sure that they don't get too tight. When your whip reaches the required height, pinch out the growing stem (generally 3ft or 1m for a standard, but you can have any height that you wish), this will encourage side shoots to form near the top. I like to try and get four good branches to form to a good head.

When these four branches are about 3–4in in length, pinching the tips encourages further branching and, with a bit of luck, you will now have your standard fuchsia. Look after it and it should give you many years of pleasure. Just one more tip, never try to grow standards as hardies and leave outside for the winter. The frost will kill the upright growth. Also when tying the plants to the canes, check all the materials you are going to use – some are not suitable as they will restrict the flow of sap and cut into the stems.

In the autumn I take my plants into the greenhouse where I have heating just above freezing point. I cut them down to about 4in. Some people think that this is rather hard, but I have done this for a number of years and I get good plants the following season. It also enables me to pack them into the greenhouse without taking up too much room.

During the dormancy period I keep plants on the dry side, then in early February, as the days start to lengthen and the sun gets a little stronger, I give them a little more water, using a spray of warm water to get the plants going. I then re-pot into a pot 1in smaller as this will help to encourage new root growth. Do this and you should soon have shoots growing and then you can start to take cuttings.

The main pests, I find, are whitefly, so try and spray every seven days, more often if you have a real problem. Remember that the spray only kills adult flies and not the eggs of larvae. Use a systemic fungicide. Red spider can be another pest. It is a sucking mite, and dry hot conditions will encourage its growth. Fuchsia rust is a fungus disease. Yellow and red spots appear over the leaves and plants that are affected are best destroyed. However, plants with isolated spots can be treated with Nimrod T. If you get a mould which appears in cold, stagnant conditions, spray with Benlate.

Feeding fuchsias is left to the individual to decide what is best for his own plants. The three main elements to be used are nitrogen, which stimulates leaf growth, phosphates for healthy root growth and strong stems, and potash to prevent soft growth and improve flower colour and size. From March to July, a fertiliser with high nitrogen is used, even Tomato Liquinure can be used for the summer months. I use Phostrogen later in the year as this has a high potash content.

The varieties of fuchsia that I would like to recommend are:

Baskets

La Campanella
Applause
Harry Grey
Powder Puff
Walsingham
Akenfield
Daisy Bell
Auntie Jinks
Pink Galore
President Margaret Stater
Romance

Standards

Border Queen
Coachman
Mrs Marshall
Mission Bells
Barbara
Mrs Lovell Swisher
Empress of Russia
Lena
Swingtime
Phyllis
Eva Boerg

Bush Types

Bealings
Charming
Genii
Achievement
Autumnale
Brutus
Fanfare
Green 'n Gold
Icecap
Sir A. Ramsey
Margaret Row
Marin Glow
Orange Drops
Pinch Me
Snow Cap
Thalia
Amy Lye
Joy Patmore
Other Fellow
Applause
Barrys Queen
Display
Golden Marinka
Hapsburgh
Lady Ramsey
Lyes Unique
Marinka
Nellie Nuttall
Orange Crush
Princess Dollar
Swanley Gem
Upward Look

These are some of the outside fuchsia that I grow, but they are not hardy.

Gardenia (Jasminoides)
The gardenia, or Cape jasmine, is a low-growing, bushy shrub and over the past few years has become a popular house plant. Some people are attracted by the richly-fragrant flowers. It rarely exceeds 20in in height or spread. The leaves are a shiny, dark green and when the flowers arrive they are mostly double white.

Gardenias do best in bright light, but not on a fully sunlit window, and a temperature of 60°F–64°F is needed when flower buds are forming. A sudden change is often the cause of buds dropping off. Try and spray plants each day with a fine mist spray and use water at room temperature – so many people lose their plants by giving them cold water. Just think how you would feel if you had to have a cold bath or cold cup of tea in the middle of winter! It all makes sense if you think about it.

Grevillea Robusta (Silly Oak)
This is a graceful pot plant to grow, with feathery foliage. I find it very useful in the winter months if I need a leaf for flower arrangements. It is grown for its foliage – and if it has flowers, I have yet to see them! One of the advantages of this specimen is that it does not require much warmth. During the summer months it can be plunged in the garden complete with pot. However, watch that it doesn't root into the ground, as it soon makes a lot of root. Grevilleas can be grown from seed, soaking the seeds first. Germination takes about four weeks in a propagator at 70°F–80°F.

Gloxinia sinningias
The proper name is *Sinningias specias,* a rare mouthful and many people would not know what you were talking about – Gloxinia is far better. This reminds me of a little, old lady who went into a shop and asked for a plant, and the shop assistant gave her the Latin name. She replied: 'Howd hud, mor. Dew you howd hud, tha's no good talkin' like a duzzy fule!'

The gloxinia can be grown from seed, sowing January to March in heat. If you are going to buy, look for one with plenty of buds, you will be able to enjoy it much longer. Gloxinia must have a light position but not strong sunlight. The secret of success with this plant, I find, is *not* to water from the top. It has a tuber (or corm) and watering can rot this.

From June to September I have a dozen gloxinia plants in my conservatory which do very well. I stand pots in pans of gravel as this helps to keep moist air circulating and a weekly dose of liquid manure is also beneficial (this is where my tank with sacks of manure juices comes in handy). The bell-shaped, velvety blooms are out of this world, in colours ranging from purple and red to white, often with spotted throats. You can save your plants from year to year. Once the flowers have died and the leaves turn yellow, reduce watering to allow the plant to dry and store in the pot until early spring at about 45°F–50°F. Then re-pot the tuber in fresh compost. Plant the hollow top of the tuber upward, or you will get new shoots underneath. (Just turn the corm over if it has been planted wrongly and no harm will be done.) Gloxinias can be propagated by leaf cuttings in early summer.

Hedera (Ivy)

If you mention ivy, some people would say 'Oh yes, any one can grow ivy'. This popular plant once had the reputation of being able to survive in any room, but they do suffer in the hot, dry air of centrally-heated homes (you will soon notice leaves going brown at the tips and edges if they are not in a happy situation).

One can have the choice of dozens of varieties, but to be successful, look for a well-clothed plant with no lengths of bare stems. Every year there are new variegated leaf forms coming out. Fibrex Nurseries, Pepworth, Stratford-on-Avon deal with hundreds of ivy of all descriptions.

Hibiscus rosa sinensis

Hibiscus, or Rose of China, is another plant that is becoming increasingly popular. Holiday-makers who have been to the tropics will have seen this plant grown by the roadside, but in this country it has only been grown successfully as an indoor plant. Originally there were only reds and pinks in the flowers, but new varieties are now available. You will find that it requires a heated room plus a humid atmosphere. The plant likes to be watered freely and given a weekly dose of liquid manure. Watch out for whitefly, they seem to like this plant. If you get bud drop, it is often due to change of temperature or under-feeding.

Hoya carnosa (Wax Flower)

Another of my favourite plants, some people also call it the plastic flower. There is another variety, 'Hoya Bella', which has a smaller leaf. The name of the plant was derived from an Englishman, Thomas Hoy, who was head gardener to the Duke of Northumberland at Syon House, Middlesex at the end of the eighteenth century.

I find the 'Carnosa' easy to grow and it makes a good plant to train round a hoop or climb up a wall. It has hard, fleshy pairs of oval leaves about 2–3in long, and the star-like flowers come in clusters of about twelve or more to a bunch. New stems are bare, the leaves appearing later (don't cut them off). When the flowers are out in abundance, the scent is breath-taking. Do leave the dead flowers on the plant as new flower buds will develop where they occur. Refrain from feeding the plant once buds have formed, otherwise the growth becomes too vigorous and you will find the buds will drop.

The pest which I find the biggest problem is the mealy bug – I take a small child's paint brush and paint with methylated spirit. It's the only thing which will kill these little white bugs as they lay eggs underneath the leaves, so have a good look round when painting.

Hoyas dislike being over-watered. I find that tap water leaves a white deposit (it's the lime in our hard water), so use rain water if you have an old 'soft water butt'.

Hydrangea macrophylla

Once again, this is an old-fashioned pot plant which many people will buy in late spring. The hydrangea is sold when in flower, and lasts in bloom for six to eight weeks. Keep it on the cool side as it dislikes a warm room; also give it plenty of water. Visitors often ask me how to turn pink varieties into blue. All you have to do is give the pink plants half a teaspoonful of alum. Once the hydrangea has flowered cut back the stems to half their height.

Impatiens (Busy Lizzie, Balsam)

You will probably know the plant much better by the name 'Busy Lizzie'; it is one of the easiest plants to take from cuttings. Take a piece of stem off the plant, pop it into a jar with some water and you should have a cutting with roots in ten days.

Impatiens are one of the most popular pot-plants of today, and are almost perpetual flowering. There have been many new varieties introduced in recent years; in fact, they are one of the easiest plants to grow, with over thirty varieties listed.

The 'Double Rosette' and 'Double Duet' are just like small rosebuds when the flower forms. Another variety I like is the 'New Guinea' with its multi-coloured leaves and much larger flowers.

Regular spraying is very necessary as whitefly and red spider can be a menace in hot weather and can also cause buds and flowers to drop. Remember, if you keep the plant pot-bound, it will help to produce more flowers. Impatiens like light but avoid direct sunlight in summer. Compost should be kept moist, but ease up on the water in winter. Impatiens can not stand the cold, and must have heat of 60°F or more in the winter. Feed once a week.

Iresine herbstii (Blood Leaf Beefsteak Plant)

This is another popular plant, with deep red leaves; even the stems are red. Another name for it is 'Chicken Gizzards'; understandable, as, looking at the leaves, one would think it was a gizzard. One thing the iresine likes is the sun. Mine do very well in the summer greenhouse, but I find that they need cutting back twice a year or one gets a leggy plant. Give plenty of water, spraying leaves regularly. Feed every two weeks.

Maranta marantaceae (Prayer Plant)

The maranta gets its name, Prayer Plant, because the leaves fold at night just like a pair of hands in prayer; it is also known as the Ten

Commandments plant. It likes to be situated in natural light.

Again there are many varieties but the *marantaceae* has olive-green leaves with red veins, purplish red underneath. Maranta do not like direct rays from the sun or cold draughts, but they do like a warm room in winter. The plant has small white or pink flowers, but they are insignificant and its main artistic value lies in the beautiful leaves. I find that they like a shallow pot instead of a deep one and like to be fed in winter as well as the summer months.

Monstera deliciosa (Swiss Cheese Plant)

This is a hardy plant with long aerial roots. If properly looked after, this plant can be enjoyed for years, but *please*, don't cut the aerial roots.

The monstera likes a warm room and a daily spraying, as it prefers to live in a damp atmosphere. Damp compost is also important plus a good feeding once a week with diluted liquid manure. Yellow leaves are often the result of over watering and if the leaves turn brown the plant may be standing too near a radiator which is too hot for it. I have seen monsteras standing in hallways with the leaves all brown and with papery edges. The usual cause of this problem is that the air is too dry; but if the tips of the leaves go brown, check for over-watering first. Aerial roots can be trained round a moss-covered pole or into the potting compost.

Pelargonium grandifiorum (Geraniums)

One of the most common of house plants and best loved flowers. As a child I remember most cottages in the villages had a large red geranium in the window. When the horses went home after working in the fields, mother used to say 'Run and shovel up the horse droppings' – these were later used to re-pot the geraniums. We also collected the soil from molehills; I don't know why, but it was thought to be the best soil to use.

I can understand why the geranium is so popular, as even a child can grow this plant. Like a lot of modern plants, there are over three hundred varieties, all due to hybridism. The best known is the 'Zonal Pelargonium' which we still call geranium. Then there is the 'Regal Pelargonium' and ivy-leaved varieties, which are becoming such favourites for use with hanging baskets. The scented-leaved geranium is lovely to use for pot pourri, and even for cooking.

I grow more of these lovely pot plants outside than in the greenhouse; but in my small conservatory, I have a few of my favourites like 'Distinction', 'Mrs Henry Cox', 'Happy Thought' and the regals like 'Dubonnet', 'Grand Slam' and 'Rembrant'. The best loved of the ivy-leaved variety are 'L'Elegante', 'Balkon Royale' and 'Yale'; but even after all these named varieties, we must not forget the super ones which we can grow from seed. The regal pelargoniums will only flower in the spring and early summer, unlike the zonal varieties which you will see in bloom for a much longer period.

The main pest of the pelargonium in the greenhouse is, of course, the whitefly. I use 'Sprayday' – but I do think pests get immune to the same spray, so it is a good idea to change from time to time, there are plenty of sprays on the market from which to make your choice.

I know a lot of people have problems in keeping geraniums over the winter months. A couple of tips: firstly, don't let them get too wet, particularly in cold conditions as this will undoubtedly lead to losses; secondly, dip the plants in a fungicide like 'ICI Benlate' before potting up, to prevent diseases attacking, and once the pots or boxes are full of plants give another good spray with Benlate, all over the plants.

Feeding geraniums is important when they are actively growing; they will need a high potash feed. Once they start to bloom, feed once a week with liquid manure.

Peperomia piperaceae

Another popular little plant, often used in bottle gardens. I like the plant because of its neatness in growing and the leaves always fascinate me. *Peperomia caperata* is a fine example with its heart-shaped leaves and rippled surface of dark green colour. The flowers look like a shepherd's crook of white spikes appearing from April to December. There are, of course, many peperomias, which in their own way all have special attractions, mostly I think for their leaves. The flowers are really nothing to talk about, but some gardeners will no doubt disagree.

To look after your plant you will need to keep it in an average temperature of 50°F to 55°F in winter. Peperomias need a bright room but not direct sunlight. I find that you need to water with care or you can soon get botrytis, or grey mould, setting in. Feed in summer months every four weeks with a weak feed (if you overfeed you will get too much soft growth).

Philodendron scandens (Sweetheart Plant)
Once more we have a tropical plant which, over the years, has become a climbing tree specimen with over 200 species to choose from. I can see why it is called the Sweetheart Plant, as its growth sends out aerial roots at each root node, which then attach themselves to the main stem, climbing like lovers. I have seen this plant trained along walls but it needs support. This is the smallest species in the philodendron group.

You will find the 'Bipinnatifidum' and 'Selloum' varieties in large offices and buildings as they are non-climbers. They are quite capable of growing into 'Grut owd plants', as we say in Suffolk (great old plants), so it would be wise to give this plant to a public home, if you own one. The Sweetheart will endure a lower heat, just 50°F, but the other varieties mentioned will need 65°F. Please don't over-water, as so many philodendrons are killed by over-watering. Just keep the soil moist in winter, and water once a week in the summer months. Give a feed every two weeks.

Pilea cadierei (Aluminium Plant)
This is also known as the water melon plant and comes originally from Indo-China. It has become very popular because, once again, it has beautiful leaves. Tiny flowers may appear but they are scarcely noticeable. Pilea is a good house plant for the beginner to grow. It requires an average warmth of 50°F in winter, and needs more water in summer than one would believe – I was surprised at how much a small plant can take, but I find it best to let pots dry out in between each good drink. Try and give the leaves a regular misting and feed every two weeks. Another little tip is to nip out

over-long shoots, as this will encourage a better, well-balanced growth to form.

Plumbago capensis (Cape Leadwort)
This is one of the prettiest climbers with its clusters of pale blue flowers from April to October. It can climb to a height of 15ft or so, but you will have to tie in its floppy stems. The plumbago does not like to be in a heated room during the winter. Leaves will often fall, but new foliage will appear when growth starts again. I like to prune my plants back in early spring, shortening all growths by two-thirds. Give it a good, weekly feed and you will be rewarded with a lot of pleasure.

Primulaceae (Primula)
'A fine winter pot plant' I was once told; *primulaceae* refers to the early flowers. There are over 500 species listed, but I shall give you the few that I have grown. *Primula obconica* or poison primrose – so called because some people can come out with a skin irritation after handling this variety. This is easy to grow, needing a weekly feed to keep the flowering period going. It can be kept from year to year, but I find that you get a much better plant with annual sowing of seed.

Primula sinensis or Chinese primrose will flower and flower. It is often called the old-fashioned plant of the primula family as so much work has been done to produce the modern hybrids. I quote from Thompson & Morgan's catalogue: 'a plant that knows no limit to its range of colours'.

Primula malacoides fairy primrose will need plenty of soft water and feeding. The removal of dead blooms prolongs the flowering period. This primula is often called the 'baby' because its small flowers grow in tiers on slender stems. Like all primulas, they will need a good light and temperature around 50°F (if the room is too warm, the flowers will drop). Keep compost moist, but don't stand pots in water. Feed once a week with liquid manure.

Rhipsalidopsis gaertneri (Easter Cactus)
At first glance you might get this cactus muddled up with the

Christmas blooms

Christmas cactus, *Zygocactus truncatus.* That's a real mouthful; we'll 'wheelbarrow' that, as my dad used to say if it was a long word.

The Easter cactus flowers in the spring. It comes from Brazil where it grows in trees, in forks of the branches. Forest cactii may not be grown in gritty compost but they should have plenty of leaf mould put into the potting compost. The flowers are bright scarlet and bell shaped. The plant should be kept growing through the autumn and winter, allowing it to rest after February by reducing the water and feeding. Once the red flower buds appear, the watering can be re-started.

I like to put my cactii outside in the summer. I stand the pots around my patio; they seem to like the sunshine and rain water, but I get them in again before October's cold night.

Remember – with Easter and Christmas cactii, once the flower buds have appeared the plants must not be moved or turned round as the buds will drop.

Rhododendron azalea obtusa

I think this must be the most misunderstood house plant. So many people fail to understand the conditions it needs to survive that it often dies within four weeks of purchase. The two varieties familiar as house plants are *Azalea simsii* and *Azalea obtusum* and many are lost because they are not given enough water (it should be soft rain water).

Azalea obtusum flowers from March to May. Daily spraying after the plant has flowered is beneficial. It does best in a cool room and can also be plunged in the garden during the summer months, but don't forget to feed and water it. Feeding is only necessary when the plant is in growth, not in full flower.

Azalea simsii is a smaller, compact plant, but has the larger flowers, being either single or double. It doesn't like a hot room so keep the temperature at 45°F to 50°F. This is often why it dies as the heat dries out the roots in the compost. Flowers will then flop and leaves drop; so do watch the heat and give them plenty of rain water (lime water will sometimes make plants chlorotic; you will notice the leaves turning yellow). Plants will do well if you stand the pots in damp pebbles for extra humidity; this can be a boon if you have centrally-heated rooms.

Saintpaulia ionantha (African violet)

All the ladies love violets, but the African violet is something special. Long gone are the days when these flowers were all blue, they now come in a variety of lovely colours. Once you have an African violet you will soon become an addict. The person we have to thank for the discovery of our *Saintpaulia* was a German, Baron Walter Von St Paul, who made his discovery in Tanganyika, (Tanzania) in 1890, and in his honour these hardy, new plants were given the botanical name of *Saintpaulia.* The violet remains true to its origin as a shade-loving tropical plant, and this is the reason why it adapts to life indoors. Given sufficient light, the plants will grow well and require little attention.

I well remember going to interview Tony Clements in his specialist nursery at Terrington St Clements, Kings Lynn, Norfolk. He told me that, in spite of what people say, African violets are the easiest of pot plants to grow. The *Saintpaulia* has four basic needs – water, light, warmth and food. Given all these, with a little bit of love and care, your plants will thrive and be a source of pleasure for years. Never water these charming, little plants until they flag; wait until the compost is dry and the plant wilts before giving any water. Tony told me that more violets are killed by over-watering, than by all the pests and diseases put together. If your plant tells you that it is thirsty, stand it in a bowl of tepid water about 2in deep. Leave it for a time, then remove the plant, let it drain and return it to its home on the windowsill or pot stand. African violets must also have light, in fact, all you can give them but of course, not direct sunshine. The ideal place is on a north-facing windowsill where they will have good light all the year round. If they have insufficient light, they will fail to flower. If you give your violets this attention, you should have some super plants. Another tip given to me by Tony was to try and keep the violets next to the glass of a window at all times. Remember that the African violet comes from tropical Africa, so you will understand that it needs warmth – sitting room or kitchen is best, with a temperature of 65°F. He also told me that the only feed he gave his plants was Phostrogen.

Cuttings can be taken easily, making sure of success by taking a healthy leaf. I put mine in water on the windowsill (or the leaves may be put in a mixture of peat and sand) and they should root in about eight weeks.

Seed can also be sown and should germinate in three weeks, but it will need heat. Using a propagator is best at a temperature of 70°F–75°F. Another point; if you are sowing seed, don't sneeze! The seed is so fine that it is very difficult to see and can easily be blown away.

My favourite African violet is the variety 'Fancy Pants', followed by 'Kristi Marie'. If you are ever in Norfolk, it is well worth a visit to Tony's nursery. I certainly enjoyed my tour and will never forget the lovely colours – I hope one day to be able to see a yellow one.

Sansevieria trifasciata (Mother-in-law's Tongue)

This is also known as snake plant. It seems so unfair to call the *Sansevieria* 'Mother-in-law's Tongue' (in the US it is known as the snakeskin plant). I suppose the leaves are sword-like and that's how it got its name. It must be the only plant which can stand in full sunshine or a shady corner, even in draughts and still survive. *Sansevieras* do flower, the erratically clustered white or yellow flowers growing on an erect spike, but they do not have a lot of perfume. The most popular variety is called 'Laurentii' – I like the yellowing edges on the leaves. The 'Zeylanica' has grey-green, cross bands on the foliage. Cuttings can be taken relatively simply: cut the adult leaves in sections of about 4in and place these in small pots with plenty of sand and peat, and eventually roots will form. I must point out that if you take cuttings of the 'Laurentii' they will only produce plain green leaves with hardly any markings and no yellowing edges. To keep the original colouring, you would have to take sections from the roots. Keep temperature to not less than 50°F, feed once a month in the winter and water about every six weeks. I find that they do much better when the plant is pot-bound. Don't re-pot until the pot bursts with its roots!

Saxifraga (stolonifera) (Mother of Thousands)

You can see why this plant has the name mother of thousands from the way it grows, with tiny, baby rosettes on thread-like stems. I think it looks like a mother hen with her brood of chicks. It has no stems as such, growing no more 8–10in high with little flower spikes of pale pink or white blooms appearing in late summer. It looks at its best hanging in a small basket or container and is decorative in the daintiest way.

Over the years a *Saxifraga* 'Tricolour' has come on to the market. Its variegated form is a little more tender and requires more warmth, and fewer young plants are produced. Cuttings are easy to take as you just peg down the plantlets on compost. I water them liberally during the growing season, but plants must not stand in water. Feed once a week and keep warm in winter at 45°F.

Solanum capsicastrum (Winter cherry)

This is a charming little plant to have at Christmas, sometimes called false Jerusalem cherry, but I would warn mothers with small children that it has berries which are poisonous. With red, orange, yellow and green fruits the size of small sweets, what could be more attractive to the little ones? It is related to the nightshade family.

Now, after the bad things, I will say what a delightful plant this is; easy to grow from seed early in the spring, producing flowers and fruit in the same year. An old gardener friend of mine had a winter cherry for years. It was in a clay pot and measured 3ft by 3ft. In the summer months it was immersed in the garden, watered and fed. Each autumn the same shrub was full of berries and it was taken back into the house at the end of September.

During the winter keep the compost moist at all times, spray with water frequently and keep at a temperature of about 50°F. After flowering and the berries have fallen, prune back the stems to half their length and re-pot (that is, if you wish to keep your plant from year to year). Personally, I find that sowing seed each year produces a better plant for the festive season. Again, *solanum* is attacked by whitefly and regular spraying is needed to combat this pest.

Stephanotis floribunda (Waxflower)

I always call this plant the 'Bride's Plant' as the flowers are marvellously scented, reminding me of a church decorated for a wedding, and these flowers are often used in the bride's bouquet. It is not the easiest of plants to grow; if not reared under ideal conditions, the leaves will soon drop. It is important to keep the temperature as constant as possible, at 65°F–70°F; this will keep the *stephanotis* happy. During active growth keep the compost moist, but ease off watering in the winter. Stand the plant on a dish of pebbles as this helps to give a moist atmosphere. Use tepid water and feed weekly.

The *stephanotis* is a twining shrub and a cane is needed for support in the first year. As the plant grows you can make a wire ring and train it into whatever shape you wish. The flowers are waxy white and very fragrant, appearing in the spring and continuing into the summer. They grow in clusters of eight or more tube-shaped blooms. Once the buds appear, don't turn the plant or move it.

A pest which sometimes can be a problem, is the scale insect, a small brown insect which makes a sticky substance on the leaves. Spray with an insecticide.

Strelitzia reginae (Bird of Paradise Flower)
I would like as many pounds as the times I have been asked the question 'Why does my bird of paradise plant have no flowers?' I would be quite rich! It is sometimes eight years or more before flowers appear, and patience is required. Root restriction is vital in helping it to bloom. So many people think 'Ah, its pot is full of roots, I will give it more room in a larger size pot'; but if you think about it, the plant will produce more foliage in this way, and lose out on the blooms.

I call the *strelitzia* the plant of patience. It can be grown from seed and takes six months or so to germination, then another eight years for a flower to appear. Just like a bird, a boat-shaped bract with flowers of bright orange and dark purple emerges looking like a heron in appearance. The stems are 2–3ft long and the leaves are leathery and dark green, sometimes 2ft in length. In winter a normal room temperature of 55°F–60°F is advisable. I stand my plants outside under the shelter of a south-facing wall in the summer, but once they are blooming I bring them back into the greenhouse. I give mine a feed each week and water, keeping compost moist, but in winter I like to keep the plants on the dry side.

Streptocarpus (Cape Primrose)
At one time, the *streptocarpus* was just a stove plant and only grown in large greenhouses. Nowadays they are grown as house plants with great success. The range of seeds is remarkable. 'Windowsill Magic' is how they are described by Thompson & Morgan in their seed catalogue. Colours range from blue to pink to white. The Cape primrose resembles a gloxinia but has no tuber, so cannot be over-wintered in dry soil. It will keep for years if you give it the right conditions. Mildew can be a problem with this plant. Don't water on the leaves, keep it rather on the dry side and cease to feed in the dormant season. The plant will need an average warmth of 55°F–60°F.

Thunbergia alata (Black-eyed Susan)
If you need a house plant to cover a large area such as a trellis, this is the plant to grow. Although actually a perennial, it is usually

treated as a house plant. I raise mine from seed in early spring, then plant them in hanging baskets where they do very well. With stakes and wire hoops all sorts of shapes can be attained with the long trailers, but once the flowers have died, it is vital to remove the dead ones or the flowering season will be curtailed. Plants can be over-wintered but they are better if seed is sown each year.

The blooms, are yellow and orange with brown centres. They need a good feed each week once the blooms arrive and the compost should be kept moist. When I grew *thunbergia* in the greenhouse I often found red spider disease was a problem.

Tolmiea menziesii (Piggy-back Plant)
Sometimes called mother of thousands or youth on age. I like this plant, especially the variegated one. It comes from America and has an interesting way in which it reproduces itself. It's called a piggy-back plant because a small plantlet grows from the joint of each leaf and stalk. This brings down the weight of the plant so it then looks as if it is trailing. The flowers are small, white and insignificant. *Tolmiea* is grown for its foliage and I feel that it is one of the hardiest of all house plants. Again, the red spider is a pest to this plant. Just keep it moist and give a standard weekly feed and your *tolmiea* will be happy!

Tradescantia fluminensis (Wandering Jew)
These well-known plants grow very well and I would expect most house plant lovers to own one or more varieties, as there is a large collection of *tradescantia.* The name is derived from the gardener of Charles I, John Tradescant. The leaves of the different varieties are small, oval and pointed, variegated cream or white with stripes, sometimes yellow or pale pink to red. They grow rapidly, and are one of the easiest plants from which to obtain cuttings.

If your *tradescantia* becomes too long, pinch out the growing points to encourage side branches. The flowers on the *tradescantia* are insignificant. Provide average warmth in winter, ease up on the watering and feed only every second month.

Zygocactus truncatus (Christmas Cactus or Thanksgiving Cactus).
The same rules apply to the Christmas cactus as the Easter cactus.

Vegetables

Here is a list of vegetables which I grow:

Artichoke (Globe)
Asparagus
Beans (Broad, Dwarf, French, Runner)
Beetroot
Beet Spinach
Brassicas
Broccoli
Carrots
Celery
Celeriac
Cucumbers
Leeks
Lettuces
Marrows and Courgettes
Onions
Parsnips
Peas
Potatoes
Radish
Swedes, Turnips and Kholrabi
Sweetcorn
Tomatoes

Artichoke (Globe)

Although belonging to the same family as the Jerusalem artichoke, this plant is quite distinct in appearance and resembles a large, coarse-growing, grey-green thistle. It is cultivated for the large, globular flower heads which should be well closed with plump, fleshy scales. It is essential to cut the flower heads before the blossoms appear, otherwise the scales will be useless to cook. I smile to myself when I look at this plant in my garden, as I think of what Culpeper had to say about it: 'They doth increase nature and doth provoke a man's veneryous actes'. (What an aphrodisiac – I shall have to try and sell plants to male visitors only!) Perhaps this is why they are grown so well and eaten in France.

My globe artichokes are grown in the herbaceous border because I love to see the fine, large leaves of grey-green foliage; they are super to use if making a large flower arrangement, such as in a church. If the flowers are left to bloom, you will get a global head of purple on a stem some 4–5ft in height, which has a most striking appearance. Artichokes like a good loam in an open situation, with large helpings of farmyard manure. It is best to split the plant up every third year, using the suckers which are produced around the old plant. Plant these in November or April, as soon as the leaves are about 9in in length.

The globe artichoke is a perennial and some say it is hardy; but I find one can lose plants in some winters, so it is as well to put a few suckers in a cold frame for safety. One old gardener told me that when he worked on a large estate the master used to tell him to put all the coal ash around the roots of the globe artichokes, as this would help to protect the crowns from frost. Watch out too for slugs, as they do love the new shoots. Young plants need to be at least 3ft apart. Globe artichokes can be grown from seed, but they take several years to reach maturity. Once your artichoke has been left to flower, it will weaken the whole plant, so you may have to re-set shoots more often. Varieties such as 'Green Globe', 'Purple Globe' and 'Vert de Laon' are highly recommended, if you can get them.

Once you have grown the Jerusalem artichoke in your garden you will have these vegetables for a number of years, because, once established, you will not get rid of them very easily. The tuberous-rooted plant is closely related to the common sunflower and resembles it in appearance. Years ago it was called the sun root and was recommended to be grown as a substitute for the potato; it is much more hardy than the potato, easily cultivated and will thrive in the poorest of soil. The propagation of this vegetable is done by planting small tubers with one or two eyes. The sets may be planted at the end of February in trenches 4–5in deep in rows 18in–2ft apart. Lifting the crop takes place round about late October onwards. The knobby tubers are lifted once the leaves on the stems have turned brown.

I have found that this vegetable makes an excellent screen or windbreak, as it can grow 9–10ft tall (an ideal cover to screen the compost heap!) Tubers can be stored in sand for the winter months, but as frost doesn't harm them, it will depend on the availability of sand. If you wish to move these vegetables around the garden, make sure that you remove all the tubers, as any that are allowed to remain will spring up where you do not wish them to grow. The Jerusalem artichoke is not to everyone's taste, but I find that they are a super vegetable for soups in the winter months. Many more people are growing them today and, since the emphasis now is on slimming, this is an ideal vegetable to eat. Recommended varieties include 'Fuseau', 'Dwarf Sunray' (smaller than other varieties) and 'Silver Skinned'.

Asparagus

Gone are the days when the gentry were the only people to grow this impressive vegetable in their gardens. The Greeks used it for medicine and the Romans ate it as a favourite food. Asparagus is imported today from distant countries, as Britain is not able to grow enough.

Once, when I was reading a very old gardening book, I saw that the directions for laying an asparagus bed were like laying the foundations for a castle! Years ago this would have been the event of a lifetime for the gardener. As you will notice by what follows, the asparagus demands long-term investment and space. This hardy perennial will take three years to get a crop (with new varieties) and it only lasts for six weeks in the year, but once you have got a good bed you should have asparagus for twenty-odd years or so. Flower arrangers should note that asparagus is *not* a foliage to cut for use with sweet peas, or other flowers come to that. You need to leave the foliage on so that those fine succulent shoots will build up to give a superb vegetable. Seeds can be sown, but you will have to wait two years or so. My advice is to buy crowns, as the new varieties will produce shoots to cut in the second year.

When planting crowns you will first need good drainage and plenty of farmyard manure (notice that I keep talking about farmyard manure because I am lucky enough to be able to get this, otherwise garden compost may be used). Also fertilise by adding Growmore. Dig a trench 1ft wide, 10in deep and place crowns 15–18in apart (spread out). It is best if the crowns are placed on mounds of soil, along the centre, and covered with soil, making sure that the roots are well spread out when soil is level. Then in autumn you can top-up the trench with well-rotted compost.

(Keep it free from weeds!) Once the foliage has grown, don't let it set the berries as, if they germinate, you will get asparagus all over the place. Only when the foliage turns yellow should it be cut down to ground level. Once the shoots appear in late spring, cut 4in high shoots until the end of June, six weeks in all.

Varieties from seed are: 'Larac', 'Lucillus', 'Martha Washington' and 'Connovers Colossal'. Varieties from crowns are: 'Suttons Perfection', 'L'orella', 'Lucillus' and 'Connovers Colossal'.

Broad beans

Long let us work,
Where the breeze blows from yon extended field,
Of blossomed Beans. Arabia cannot boast
A fuller gale of Joy, that liberal thence
Breathes through the sense and takes the ravished soul
James Thomson

A lot of people turn up their noses at the broad bean. I know they are not so popular as the dwarf and runner beans, but put a row in early and gather the pods while they are young and you will find they are smashing. The pods may be cooked when young, as well as the beans. My father used to like them when the skins were tough and centres floury (and I used to say 'What! cook them even with black toe nails on!)

The broad bean goes back a long way; it is one of the oldest cultivated vegetables and was well known to the ancient Egyptians and Romans, but they did not think much of this bean – the Egyptians used to say that it was unclean. The poor flower bloom of the bean used to carry a supersition that if one fell asleep in a field of beans it would cause madness.

For the new gardener this vegetable must be one of the easiest to grow, and of all the bean family, the broad bean freezes the best.

Candlemas Day stick Beans in the Clay
(2 February)

I find that if broad beans are sown early there is less chance of getting blackfly, which is the most dreaded pest of this crop. There is a saying that beans sown in November will have pods fit to eat much earlier than those sown in March. I have tried both ways and it could make five to seven days difference. It cuts both ways, autumn sowings risk the plants being killed off if there is a severe winter, on the other hand, cropping will be earlier and then we are up against the blackfly. I like to sow five rows of broad beans, 1ft from row to row, planting seeds 6in apart and 2in deep. Once the plants are 4ft high I go along with a pair of hedging shears and cut 3–4in out of the tops. Doing this will help to prevent the blackfly, as they like the tenderest shoots. The tops may be cooked like spinach and eaten with a cheese sauce – 'smashing'. My late husband used to say: 'the beans will swell now that the tops have been cut off'. My brother Ronnie helps me nowadays and we put stakes at each end of the rows and tie two or three rows of twine round the beans to prevent them blowing over if there are strong winds.

There are various varieties. 'Longpods' are the hardiest and I find that they give the biggest yields. 'Aquadulce' is the best winter planted variety. 'Imperial Green Pod', 'Relon', 'Imperial White Pod', 'Bunyards Exhibition', 'Masterpiece Longpod', 'Express' and 'Witkiem Major' are other popular varieties. The pods of the Windsor varieties 'Green Windsor', 'White Windsor' are shorter and broader, and are not suitable for autumn sowing. They also take a little longer to mature. Dwarf varieties, such as 'The Sutton' (white) and 'Bonny Lad', are the beans to grow if you only have small gardens, or if you wish to grow under cloches.

Pests As I have mentioned, the blackfly is a serious pest. You can spray your plants with washing-up liquid. I fill a gallon sprayer with water, then put in 2–3 teaspoons Fairy Liquid with a dash of Jeyes Fluid and spray the beans thoroughly. (My father used old washing-up water in days gone by, with only washing soda added.) For modern pesticides, use ICI Rapid or Crop Saver. Another serious disease is chocolate spot. Small brown spots appear on the leaves and dark streaks along the stems. If the plants are badly affected, the only remedy is to destroy them. One way to prevent this, is not to grow the beans too closely together and to put plenty of good compost, muck or Growmore in the soil before planting.

Dwarf or French beans

This bean has changed its name in the last few years – when it was introduced in 1509 to Britain from the Netherlands, it was called the 'White Dutch Bean'. Nowadays we have tall- and short-growing varieties. The dwarf bean, as I shall call it, is so useful to grow if you are short of space. An excellent vegetable, it will produce a large crop from a small space. I find, as with most beans, you must gather every two or three days, otherwise they will go to seed and stop producing. So, if you are going on holiday when the beans are at the picking stage, get your neighbours to help themselves and there will still be some for you to pick for the freezer on your return.

As a rule, seeds are sown too thickly (I know, as I have done this myself, but as they come up I thin them out). If they are left too thick the whole crop suffers. Just like runner beans, they like to feel the air around them. Another good point about the dwarf bean is that early crops may be obtained by sowing a few beans in a pot in the greenhouse at the end of January. In an 8in pot sow a bean 1in deep – but you will need a temperature of 55°F during the day and not less than 41°F at night. A welcome vegetable for early spring.

The dwarf bean likes a good, open, sunny spot with plenty of well-rotted compost dug in the soil in the autumn. Never let the beans go dry at the roots as all beans like plenty of water. There are many varieties of dwarf bean, including climbing ones. I never bother about growing the variety of climbing French bean as I would rather have the runner bean. Beans also dislike cold weather and wind, so never plant in cold, wet soil as the plant will only rot. April is the time to sow in open ground, then cover with a cloche. If no cloches are available, it is better to wait until early May. It is an excellent vegetable to freeze (better than the runner bean). Here are a few varieties which I have grown and like, but there are plenty more for you to try.

'Limelight' – this is a very early bean with flat pods.

'Loch Ness' – round pods.

'Masterpiece' – semi-flat pods.

'Remus' – (a Thompson & Morgan introduction). Round pods.

This is my favourite for freezing. The pods grow above the foliage, are easier to pick, and you don't get dirty beans.

If you need a bean for the show bench, it must be 'The Prince'.

Runner bean

Out of all the vegetables this must be my favourite. Not only is it an excellent vegetable, but a fine plant which can be grown effectively in the back of a flower border, as the flowers are so pretty. Over the last few years there has been a problem about the flowers 'setting', losing the blooms and no pods forming. Sometimes too much nitrogen in the soil can result in lush foliage with flowers failing to 'set'. Applying sulphate of potash will help with this problem; 2oz per sq yd forked into the soil before planting the beans.

One can never spend too much time in preparing the ground for the runner bean. My brother digs our trench out at the end of November, 2½–3ft wide, 12–18in deep. The bottom is forked over well so that it is not too firm. A layer of farmyard muck is put in the bottom and the trench is left open until the end of February or early March. All sorts of rubbish is then put in the trench – old leaves, droppings from the chicken hut when this is cleaned out, even old newspapers; in fact you would be surprised at what does go into my trench. The only thing I don't put in is potato peelings, as they may grow.

Runner beans are grown in various ways. One is to sow in rows, then pinch out the tops at the second or third joint. Watch this closely as other running shoots will have to be pinched out too. If you neglect this job, you will get all foliage and no beans. My way of growing is 2 rows, 2½ft apart and beans planted 12–14in from plant to plant. Tall canes are fixed by crossing and tying at the top. The canes should be 8ft tall, 1ft in the ground leaving 7ft for the beans to climb. Years ago we cut hazel sticks from the hedgerows or woods, but those days are gone. I don't plant my beans straight into the soil. They are started in pots early in April (one to a pot), then planted near each cane once frost warnings are over; but – a most important point – never plant until they have been hardened-off. This means putting them outside in the daytime and getting them back in the greenhouse in the evenings. Do this for a week, then they should be ready to plant out. Beans don't like wind, so protect them if a gale arises. Varieties which I have grown and can recommend are 'Achievement', 'Enorma', 'Streamline', 'Sunset', 'Crusader', 'Prizewinner' and 'Painted Lady'.

Beetroot

Beetroot was cultivated on a large scale years ago for cattle food. Experiments for table use found that the purple- and crimson-fleshed varieties were rich in flavour. The Greeks held the beetroot in such esteem that they offered it to Apollo on silver, in his temple at Delphi. Culpeper assures us that juice from the white beet is good for the liver, spleen and headaches. He also said of the red beet: 'it would clear the head and help the hearing'; but I think the Russians have the best idea of all, as they make some of the best soups out of the beetroot called 'Borshch'.

The beetroot is an invaluable vegetable to me as I use the roots for salads, chutneys, wine-making and pickling, and the tops for flower arranging. (A good tip when cooking beetroot – if the roots are damaged when lifting them from the soil, dip them in flour, as beetroot bleed when damaged and flour will prevent this happening.) Beet require an exposed, sunny situation; they don't like growing in the shade. A rich, open soil and sandy loam produces nice clean roots. Fresh, manured soil is not good as the roots will go 'fangey' or forked. The secret with beetroot is to sow at monthly intervals, you get good sized beetroot throughout the season in this way. Late April or early May is the best time to sow maincrop. If sown earlier there is a danger of the plants 'bolting' to seed. I plant mine in drills 1ft apart and 1½in deep. You will find beetroot don't transplant well but gaps may be filled by transplanting the seedlings on a dull, showery day.

I store beet like carrots. Having two old tin baths, I put in a layer of old grow-bag contents (must be dry), then a layer of beet until the baths are full. You should have beetroot to last right up to May of the following year. One other thing, do wring the tops off, never cut them as they will bleed and lose their colour.

There is a choice of varieties. Long beetroot are not so popular with the housewife, they are mostly grown by the flower show exhibitor. I have grown the yellow and white varieties and they are very nice in salads (you don't get the stain of red vinegar if you drop some on the tablecloth!)

I grow beet spinach; (in some catalogues it goes under the name of perpetual spinach) using only the tops. This does not go to seed like ordinary spinach, it is very succulent, very hardy and indispensable for a winter vegetable. But I do find that the sparrows will pick at it in my garden.

Swiss chard is another form of beet, but one grown for its foliage. This vegetable has two uses; the green foliage can be cooked like spinach, and the stems (which are white and like celery to look at) may be cooked as a second vegetable and – as with asparagus – served with butter, 'it's super'.

If you are interested in flower arranging, don't forget to grow some of the rainbow chard, the colours are 'out of this world'. Put a few plants in your flower garden to create a point of interest. Its technicolour mixture of red, yellow, purple and white is unbelievable. Swiss chard is not grown nearly enough in our cottage gardens, I feel, especially as its vitamin content is so high. After a late summer crop it dies down to ground level, but as soon as spring arrives (early March) it will burst into growth for another excellent crop. Varieties are:

Red beetroot – 'Boltardy' (a good variety, resistant to running to seed), 'Detroit Lora', 'Monopoly' and 'Crimson Globe' (still a favourite with the old gardeners).

White beetroot – Albina vereduna.

Yellow beetroot – Burpees golden.

Brassica

Another little tip – never put brassica stalks in the compost heap as they are full of disease and they don't rot down easily. I let mine stand upright at the top of the garden till nice and dry, then burn them.

On the subject of disease, I think that club-root (*Plasmodiophora brassicae*) is one of the worst diseases to have in the garden. The fungus lives in the soil in the form of nesting spores, surviving for many years. The disease can be spread by contaminated soil or introduced on already infected roots of young plants bought for transplanting. You will soon notice if your plants have contracted this disease. The first sign, on a hot day, is that the plant suddenly collapses; it appears stunted and may die completely. If you pull the root up, you will find it swollen and distorted, and the leaves will be yellow. (This disease also affects the wallflower family). To avoid this, raise the seedlings in sterilised soil and dip the roots in a solution of Club Root Dip, Calomel or Benlate plus Jeyes Fluid. I use a lot of Jeyes around the garden but you have to learn not to be too heavy-handed and put extra spoonfuls in your bucket or sprayer, especially if you are putting it on greens or peas, as it will burn the foliage. I use 1 teaspoonful to 2 gallons of water – this is enough to keep birds from eating the vegetables; the smell helps to keep them at bay.

The brassicas which I like to grow are as follows:

Broccoli Purple and white sprouting. What a joy it is to have this vegetable after the cold winter. Suddenly little spears of sprouting broccoli appear. So many people make the mistake of overcooking broccoli, it should be steamed for the best flavour. It is also good for freezing.

Brussels sprouts come next and, like all the brassicae family, they can take all the muck in the soil that you can give them. My golden rule is always to have firm soil to plant sprouts in; you need not dig the land beforehand, but clean it first. One of the queries which I often get asked is 'why do my Brussels sprouts have leafy sprouts instead of hard buttons?' The cause is usually that plants were put into loose soil and were not given enough muck! Choose F^1 hybrid variety and give it plenty of water in a dry summer. I used to grow Cambridge No 5 but this is not so popular now, so I plant 'Citadel' which is not a large button variety but will last well into the winter. 'Achilles' is a heavy cropper but I find, on my heavy soil that it has a habit of falling over, so I often have to stake and tie it up. A new variety is 'Widgeon' which I have seen a lot on show benches and the flavour is very good.

One good tip with sprouts which I would like to pass on is: if you are growing the seed in the greenhouse, do try pricking out the seedlings into 3in pots (they just don't like their roots disturbed). My father used to sow his seed at the end of April, but I sow mine in early March in the greenhouse, as I find they do need that extra-long growing period.

Please do not overcook and if you wish to get rid of the smell when cooking, try putting two bay leaves into the water. Have you ever thought of pickling Brussels sprouts? Just like the pickled onion, they are very good!

Cabbage is the next on my list; another vegetable I would hate to be without. The Egyptians used to worship it! You can have cabbages all the year round, by successive sowing and transplanting. They like good soil with plenty of lime and nitrogen, plus ample watering when growing – but this is not the case when cooking! Try cooking cabbage by shredding it into very little water, shaking the pan occasionally over the heat. Cook for 10–15 minutes only and drain off the water (don't throw the water away – try drinking it with a pinch of salt and pepper; it is very good as it is full of vitamins). The cabbage can be cooked by many different methods; steaming, boiling, baking, braising and stir fry. It's a godsend to slimmers who love to make coleslaw salads. I am often surprised to see the price of the Dutch-type hard cabbage in the shops when they are such an easy vegetable to grow.

The *Chinese cabbage* is very popular; I like to eat it raw. This is another vegetable that does need watering well in dry weather. It also has the problem of 'bolting'. Now the new gardener will say 'what on earth is bolting?' This is when the middle of the cabbage looks as if it going to burst and the whole centre as if it is sending out flower shoots. An old tip which my father used to stop bolting, was to carefully split the stem with a sharp knife and wedge a matchstick (or small piece of wood of similar size) in the stalk. I think that the reason for this was to give the cabbage a shock and prevent it carrying on bolting. He also used to do this with red cabbages.

The cabbage season starts with me in early January, as I sow in the greenhouse – 'Golden Acre', a good, compact and round, firm cabbage. 'Hispi' is a very early variety; it has taken over from 'Greyhound' and will stand a long time before splitting. Gardeners who only wish for a dozen or so plants should try 'Minicole'. I also grow 'Winnigstade', this is an old favourite with flower show exhibitors as it grows to a large, pointed head and can be cut in the autumn months. After sowing the first two varieties which I mentioned in January, I plant out in the middle of April and can then cut a cabbage round about late June. My red cabbages are also sown in January and planted out in April. For winter cabbages I choose 'January King', which, to my mind is still the best cabbage for the coldest months of the year, as it stands the bad weather so well. If you go to buy this at the shops, you would be able to pick it out by the red tinge on the centre of the leaves. Winter cabbages should be sown outside in late April and transplanted in late June, ready for cutting from November onwards.

The *Savoy* is easily recognisable by its curly and crisp leaves. It is another winter cabbage with an extra-long harvesting span. I have had some standing in the garden right up to April.

Now for the spring cabbages. I sow my seed in the garden the third week in August and transplant in October. 'Spring Hero' has taken over from the 'Offenham Flower of Spring', the variety which is years old. 'Spring Hero' is a much tighter round and produces heads of 2–3lb in weight. This is a big breakthrough with spring cabbage, as so often you get rather loose leaves and not much heart. I can recommend 'April' for small compact cabbages, also 'Durham Early'. When transplanting spring cabbages, I plant mine more closely than recommended (6in apart) so that I can pull a few greens early when there are no other green vegetables about, about March time.

Calabrese For the last few years I have enjoyed this much underrated vegetable. Do try 'Romanesco' – I call this the poor man's asparagus. Again, try steaming it.

Cauliflower To get good cauliflowers, you should have a nice, open, sunny site, but sheltered from winds. They need a deep, well-structured soil with good drainage, but never let them suffer from lack of water. They also need plenty of farmyard manure (if you can get it!) Much depends on the spacing of the plants. I like to put my plants out 18in apart for summer varieties and 20–24in for winter varieties, and 2ft from row to row. I stagger the rows, planting the cauliflowers in the second row diagonally to those in the previous row; you can get more plants in each row in this way. In a dry summer do water the plants well; but if water is in short supply, limit it to heavy watering when the curds have just started to form, 3–4 weeks before picking.

Kale is another under-rated vegetable. My father never grew this, but with new tastes more and more people are growing kale, as I have found when going around judging gardens. The curly-leaved variety is the most popular. Each leaf has a frilled and curled edge looking quite like parsley. Another good thing about growing kale, unlike the rest of the brassicas, is that it will tolerate poor soil conditions, and I find that even the pigeons don't seem to touch it in my garden. I like to grow 'Dwarf Green Curled' and 'Pentland Brigg'. This variety is a little different from other kales as it is not so curly and you can get two pickings. Pick the leaves in November and again in spring when you get more sideshoots; a good stand-by vegetable when not much else is available.

Brassicae Varieties

Broccoli		Early Purple Sprouting
		White Sprouting
	Annuals	Calabrese Green Comet
		Romanesco
	Perennial	Nine Star Perennial (Never let flowerheads open and then you will obtain small heads year after year.)
Brussels Sprouts	F[1] hybrid	Peer Gynt
		Achilles
		Welland
		Widgeon
		Citadel
	Standard	Cambridge No 5
		Bedford

Cabbage	Spring	Durham Early
		Spring Hero
		Harbinger
		April
		Offenham Flower of Spring
	Summer	Minicole
		Primo
		Golden Acre
		Hispi
		Winnigstadt
		Greyhound
	Winter	January King
		Christmas Drumhead
	Savoy	Ormskirk
		Savoy King
		Best of All
	Red cabbage	Red Drumhead
		Ruby Ball
	Chinese cabbage	Two Seasons
		Tip Top
Cauliflower	Summer	All the year round
		Dok-Elgon
		Snowball
		Dominant
	Autumn	Autumn Giant
		Barrier Reef
		Canberra
	Winter	St Agnes
		Angers No 2
		Purple Cap (something different)
Kale	Curly leaved	Dwarf Green Curled
		Spurt
	Plain leaved	Cottagers
		Thousand Headed
	Leaf spear	Pentland Brigg

Carrots

I have been told that the British people eat more carrots than any other nation in Europe; no wonder, as they are such a versatile vegetable. What's a joint of boiled beef without carrots! Years ago the wild carrot was used in many medicines, one of which was for the healing of wounds. The Greeks called the carrot the love root as they believed it to possess the powers of love and passion. There is still the tale that if you eat raw carrot it will improve the eyesight. Carrots are rich in sugar and also contain vitamins B, C, D and E. They are best eaten raw because the vitamins are destroyed by cooking – the skin contains the greatest amount of vitamins.

So many gardens today are small handkerchief size that the smaller varieties of carrot, like 'Suko', 'Kundulus' and 'Amsterdam Forcing' are grown. When I go around to judge at the flower shows I always admire a good class of carrot as they surely must be the most difficult vegetable to present, looking at their best. There may be excellent tops above the ground, but below soil level it may be totally different and no one can guarantee what success will come out of the soil as the carrot is pulled up.

This vegetable thrives best in deep, rather sandy soil and is preferably grown on land which has been well-manured for a different crop the previous year. The ground should be well dug in the winter (if you plant on newly-manured ground you will get very forked or fanged carrots). Seeds are sown round about the end of March and I always put a few radish seeds in with the carrots. The radish comes up first enabling you to see the rows (much easier for hoeing). I plant seeds in rows 12in from row to row, first going over the ground with a weak solution of Jeyes Fluid. If you should get the dreaded pest, carrotfly, it's worth sprinkling some Bromophos into the trench when sowing the seed. The carrotfly is a pest for which there seems to be no treatment, but you can help to prevent it. My father used to have a paraffin rag tied on a stick and walked down each row, soaking the ground with the paraffin. I use a coarse rag, soak it well and drag it along the rows. The smell is supposed to keep the fly away. Carrot splitting, as I call it, can occur when you take up the carrots. The cause is heavy rain or sudden watering after a long dry spell. There is no treatment for this and these carrots should not be stored, but used first. The housewife doesn't like to see carrots with green tops, if the top of the root has about 1½in of green it will put her off cooking that part of the vegetable. They are not harmful; the green top is caused by sunlight getting to the carrot as it is growing, but this can be easily prevented by earthing up the root as it grows. If you enter your carrots in a flower show, points would be lost for having green tops.

On the subject of flower shows, I expect some of you wonder how the exhibitor gets those lovely, straight carrots seen on the benches. First you need soil free from stones etc. For this you can either drill a row out in the garden and then go along boring holes with a crowbar 18in–24in deep and not less than 4in in diameter. Then sift a mixture of soil, peat, sharp sand and bone meal and ram the mixture into the holes *moderately* firmly, with a small rammer (don't overdo it). Sow two or three seeds in each hole and as they grow to about 2in in height, pull the weakest out leaving one seedling – you should get a few good carrots growing in this way. Or, the other way is to use, like I have done, old forty- gallon oil drums filled with good, sifted soil, sand, peat and bonemeal – but this is a back-aching job. I also grow parsnips in this way, but only for exhibition purposes because it's so hard on my poor, old back sifting all that soil! Varieties which I grow, apart from those already mentioned, are 'Autumn King' (good for winter storage), 'Chantenay', 'Red Cored' and 'Zino'. 'St Valery' is good for exhibition. Don't forget that you can make good carrot wine, jam, cake, puddings and biscuits – and even the tops can be cooked!

Celery

What can you wish to have for better flavouring than celery? This crisp, delicious salad plant reminds me so much of my childhood Sunday teas. My father was always so proud of his celery and on Sunday morning he would dig up a good head or root from the celery trench. This was then washed well and eaten raw with a piece of cheese and apple – it was a rare Sunday treat!

Celery was used medicinally years ago and was held to cure a number of ills. It is rich in minerals and vitamins. The tops of this vegetable are also edible, but alas they are usually thrown away today as it is not widely known that they are so good for use in stews and soups. Celery is good for rheumatism, it attacks fevers, is a powerful aperient; in fact, a tonic for all those who are often under the weather.

There is another old saying: 'If women only knew what celery did for men, they would wish for it at every meal'! Celery, it seems, is another aphrodisiac; the Romans used it in love potions. My word!, the Greeks and Romans must have had some 'rum' love potions as nearly all vegetables had some aphrodisiac quality. I wonder if they worked?

Growing trench celery is a definite challenge, for you will need to blanch it as well as keeping the slugs at bay. Self-blanching celery may also be grown; it is not so hardy and should be lifted before the frost. Sow the seed in early February in heat. The compost should be of a fairly rich nature. Sow seed thinly in pans or small seed trays. As soon as seedlings are large enough to handle, they should be pricked-out into larger seed trays and placed in moderate heat. Celery can't stand being checked so keep in an even temperature. Plant out in seed boxes about 3in apart. The plant should be ready to put out in trenches at the end of May. Dig a trench about 18in wide and 12in deep. Fork over the bottom of the trench to make sure that you have good drainage then put in a good layer of well-rotted manure about 3–4in deep. Return about 4–6in soil to the trench, which is now ready for the plants, setting them 8in apart.

Celery needs plenty of water in the growing season, otherwise it will bolt. Start to blanch the celery in the old-fashioned way in late summer when the plants are about 14in high, making sure that there are no slugs about. Wrap each stick of celery with old, brown paper bags (the kind potatoes come in are ideal) cut into squares and tie up with raffia to keep the soil from between the stalks. Gradually mound the soil around the plants and carry on mounding until just the tops of the leaves (about 6in) are showing. My brother pats the sides of the trench with the back of the spade so this will throw the rain off. All varieties of celery dislike sunshine and they can't take drought. When my father planted his celery trench, my brother and I had to pick branches from the hedgerows and father laid these across the trench to keep the sun off the newly-planted celery. (They were left on for about ten days or so.)

Self-blanching varieties are not so hardy as trench varieties. I like to grow mine in blocks 9in by 9in. It is best to use a cold frame for this vegetable. No earthing is necessary but all suckers should be removed as they appear. These varieties should be used before the frost comes or you may lose the crop all in one go!

Varieties to grow for trenching are 'Giant Red', 'Giant White' and 'Solid White' (Suttons), Self-blanching varieties are 'Golden Self-blanching' and 'American Green'.

Celeriac

I cannot understand why more people don't grow this fine vegetable; it is very popular on the Continent. Having a turnip root, celeriac is rather knobby but so easy to grow, not at all like celery. It is rather a slow-growing vegetable, so start it off in the greenhouse. Just like celery, it appreciates good ground. Plant out 12in apart, watching out for slugs. I lift the roots in late autumn, as with beetroot, and store them in the same way. Celeriac is very useful in soups and stews, and I grate my roots to use in winter salads – a godsend when one is short of a vegetable in the cold winter months.

Cucumber

In Victorian times the highlight of summer tea parties was cucumber sandwiches. In modern times the cucumber is used for skin tonics, lotions, eye baths and most probably in salads. The summer months are the time for this vegetable. Some people think it is indigestible. I well remember old Doctor Keer calling on me one day as I was cutting up a cucumber for a salad. He asked if I was going to soak it in vinegar, and when I replied 'Yes' he said to leave it overnight and then throw it all 'abroad' (out of doors) next day. He clearly did not think much of the cucumber; I was 'hully stammed' (amazed).

To grow the cucumber is an art in itself. If you are growing a greenhouse variety you can get all female plants, which have definite advantages. They have only female flowers so no male flowers have to be removed. If male flowers are left on the plant, it will turn the fruits bitter. Also gone are the days when cucumbers had to be grown on hot beds, when heat was obtained in greenhouses filled with dung mixed well and turned till the heap was fermented. The beds were about 4ft high and heat was in the eighties; after the beds had settled the plants were put on the top. But, to get back to present times – and the range of modern hybrids – one still needs heat to grow indoor cucumbers, but not up into the eighties.

These vegetables can be divided into two types, the greenhouse and frame cucumber. As I have stated, greenhouse cucumbers will need heat, but the frame varieties will not require the high temperatures and humid conditions required by the greenhouse type. The frame cucumber, or as we call them, ridge cues, are shorter and the skin is rougher. The flavour is about the same as greenhouse ones.

Sow your Cucumbers in March,
You will need neither bag or sack,
Sow them in April, you will have few,
I will sow mine in May,
And I will have more than you.

In the United States some old gardeners were convinced that good cucumbers will only come if seed is sown before daylight on 1st May. Cucumbers must never be allowed to suffer from lack of moisture at the roots – this is where the tank with the sackful of muck comes in handy, as you have plenty of weak, liquid feed on hand. The modern way of growing cucumbers is by the use of grow-bags. I start mine off in late spring, sowing seed individually in 3in peat pots; I like these pots and you can plant right into the compost with no root disturbance. Try to remember to sow your seeds on their sides about ½in deep. Pop them into your propagator at 70°F. You will find germination will take place in about a week. Once the plant has hardened off (do this carefully as a sudden spell of cold will upset the plant), put two to a grow-bag, making sure that the compost or surrounding soil is damp. Put a cane in the container before planting the cucumber, then you won't upset the roots. Some training of the plant is essential but let the main stem grow naturally. I tie this to the cane and then put two or three strands of wire across the greenhouse, twisting this around the cane so I end up with 12 by 12in squares. I have even used an old piece of pig netting to make a frame on which to tie the cucumber laterals.

As the main stem grows, the side shoots are trained to grow horizontally on either side of the main stem, then the growing tip is pinched out after the second leaf has formed on these lateral shoots. You can let the cucumbers grow on these side shoots. If the plant is growing well, cucumbers may be left to grow on the main stem as long as fruit is being produced.

Frame or ridge cucumbers are grown in a different way, by pinching out the growing tip after about the eighth leaf is produced, letting the side shoots grow until the sixth leaf is produced and then stopping it. You will find that your ridge cucumbers will soon bear fruit on the side shoots. Spray in dry weather if planted in the garden or frame. My father used to plant his ridge cucumbers with the Brussels sprouts – as they grew the leaves provided shade for the cucumbers. (By the way, there is no need to take male flowers from ridge varieties, because they must be pollinated if they are to crop.)

Red spider mite must be the most troublesome pest on cucumbers; you will see the leaves start to go white and crisp, just as if they have been bleached. The mites are green in summer, red in winter and a magnifying glass will soon show them up. The treatment for destroying this pest is to try and keep a damp atmosphere and spray with Malathion.

Our England is a Garden,
And such gardens are not made,
By saying Oh! how beautiful,
And living in the shade,
While better men than we, go out
In their daily lives,
Digging weeds from Garden Paths,
With broken Dinner Knives

Varieties that I have grown include greenhouse types (ordinary): 'Telegraph' and 'Conqueror'; all female varieties: 'Uniflora D F1', 'Fembaby F1' and 'Mildana F1'; outdoor varieties: 'Burpless', 'Tasty Green', 'Patio Pik' and 'Crystal Apple' (this is an unusual small, round, yellow variety; it looks just like an apple and it grows and tastes just as nice!)

Leeks

The leek is the national emblem of Wales, but its horticultural heart lies in the north-eastern counties of England. It is the pot leek in that part of the world, but I have seen some very good leeks grown in my part of the country. They are easy to grow and another of winter's best standby vegetables. Just grow them like onions in seed trays in the greenhouse in January. Plant out at the end of April for a few early specimens, and also if you need some for exhibition. As a rule, most gardeners plant leeks out where the first early potatoes are lifted from the ground. When leeks are 6–8in high and as thick as a pencil, mark out your rows and plant 1ft apart, making holes with a dibber 6in round and 8in apart, first cutting the root ends and leaf tips to about 1in. The sparrows love to pull out leeks, and you often have to re-plant the next day.

Varieties which I grow are 'Catalina', 'Prizetaker' and 'Musselburgh'. Leeks are planted in holes in the soil so that, as they grow, you get that nice, long, blanched white root. If you wish to produce leeks for exhibition, try growing some in 6in diameter land drains. You won't have to earth them up and in this way they will grow larger and be in a good condition for the show. Do give them a feed of Phostrogen, administered as a root or foliar feed; one teaspoonful to one gallon of water, twice a week.

Remember that the same instructions apply to leeks as to onions – if you have diseased soil, for example smut, black spots and blotches will appear on the leaves and bulbs. Only the young plants are affected, the leaves becoming thickened and twisted. If orange spots and blotches appear on the surface of the leaves it is probably rust. This problem is uncommon, but the effect can be fatal in a severe attack in summer. White tip is another problem that can turn leaf tips of leeks white and papery in autumn. Disease spreads downwards and growth is stunted.

To make leek milk slice and wash the green tops thoroughly, cover with milk and simmer until tender. Season lightly and drink hot for a cold cure.

Lettuce

Lettuce is one of our oldest vegetables; they were first mentioned in writing in the seventh century. Lettuce was used to cure ulcers on the eyes and as a medicine for dropsy. In King Alfred's day, it was said that the sign of the cross should be made when cutting a lettuce, otherwise one would be possessed of the devil. (The devil was supposed to be sitting in the lettuce.)

Years ago, when we were children, lettuces were only grown in the summer, plus one at Christmas. However, the amateur can now grow a suitable selection of varieties all the year round, with a little help from frames and cloching. This slimmer's vegetable must have plenty of water during the dry period of growing and plenty of nitrogen, so get the ground well prepared. Another important point is that not all lettuce seeds germinate at the same time; much will depend on the conditions and temperature of the soil, so try different varieties.

The one which took the visitors' eye in my garden this last year or so, has been the variety called 'Continuity', a cabbage type best sown in spring and early summer. It is long-standing and reddish-brown in colour, and the birds don't seem to attack it like they do the green varieties – as soon as you put a row of green lettuce plants out, the birds are after them, I can only think that it is the tender, lush leaves which they like.

There are four types of lettuce to grow: loose leaf, cabbage crisphead, butterhead and cos. Slugs love lettuce and they are a real menace – I have seen a row of plants eaten off in one night. Botrytis can be a problem if grown under glass, the disease being encouraged by low temperature and high humidity. Bolting or running-to-seed is another problem. The cause is often a check in the growth at some stage of the plant's life, or being left in the seed trays for too long a period. The following are some types which I have grown:

Cos: 'Little Gem' (this speaks for itself, a godsend for small gardens), 'Winter Density', 'Romance' and 'Erthel'.
Butterhead: All the year round', 'Hilde', 'Arctic King', 'Kwiek' and 'Susan'.
Crisphead: 'Iceberg', 'Webbs Wonderful' and 'Great Lakes'.
Looseleaf: 'Salad Bowl'.

Marrow, Courgette and Pumpkin

These vegetable are all grown in the same way. But, one thing I would say is, that they take more farmyard manure than any other vegetables grown; they really do thrive on it. As a child I well remember that all my father's farmyard muck (muckle as we called it) was neatly stacked at the top of the garden with about 3–4in of soil spread on the top of the heap, and two 'rare grut' (great) marrows growing down – he had some 'rum' marrows (good ones).

These vegetables all belong to the cucurbit family. Courgettes are baby marrows and ideally, if you choose a small-growing marrow, this is what you will get. It is only over the last few years that the courgette has come into fashion – a result, I suspect, of so many people going to the Continent for holidays as it is very much grown and used over there. The Americans love this vegetable too; also the 'squash', another form of the marrow family, which has hard skin but soft flesh.

Seed should be sown in small pots towards the end of April in warmth. Plant out at the end of May and protect against frost. Give plenty of water during any dry period.

Varieties of marrow are: 'Zucchini', 'Blondy', 'Green Bush' and 'Small Pak'. Trailing types are: 'Table Dainty' and 'Long Green'. A variety of squash is vegetable spaghetti and hundredweight is a variety of pumpkin.

One hint passed on to me is to grow nasturtiums with marrows as they help to keep aphids away and are also supposed to improve the flavour of the marrows – or courgettes.

Onion

The onion is good for the heart. Researchers have reported, as a result of studies, that the essential oils of both onions and garlic help to reduce the level of cholesterol in the blood. Eating garlic, or hanging a bulb around your neck, should help to protect you from germs. Culpeper says 'A remedy for all diseases'.

The shallot is a small type of onion. It has many uses and can be grown to be used like a spring onion. The bulb part is reddish-brown in colour with purplish-white cloves beneath the outer skin. The shallot has a mild, faintly garlic flavour, and grows in clumps of four to five bulbs. When cooking shallots, they should not be browned as they will become bitter. When we were small, my mother would toast a shallot on a fork until hot, wrap it in an old piece of cloth and put it in our ears if we suffered from earache; this was supposed to be a cure. Once the small onion was put in the ear, you forgot the pain for the shallot was so hot that it burned your ear!

Chives are another important member of the onion family, but they have a much milder flavour which makes them a superb seasoning for a number of dishes. Chives make a good edging plant and an excellent container and indoor plant.

There are also the 'Welsh' and 'Everlasting' onions, which are hardy, perennial, evergreen onions. These are grown in clumps like the chives.

Onions are my favourite vegetable to grow. Once you have developed a good onion bed, you keep it. But if you get any of the following diseases do change your bed; it's not worth trying to grow any of the onion family, on disease ridden soil – neck rot (grey mould appearing near neck); white rot (foliage turns yellow and wilts. White mould appears on the base of the bulb) or shanking (centre leaves turn yellow and collapse. Outside leaves soon follow). The onion always enjoys a good feed, so when you are preparing the bed dig in plenty of good manure (or cow muck). Make sure that your land has ample lime in the soil. If you are not certain, try this old tip with a saucer of vinegar. Drop a piece of the soil in the vinegar, and if it starts to bubble away, you can be sure that the soil has plenty of lime. If there is not a bubble in sight, give the soil 4oz of lime to the square yard. I also like to work into my onion bed, 4oz wood ash and 2oz old soot to every square yard. You need to tread the soil firmly, raking level and then rolling it.

Onions must have firm soil to push against when they heave themselves out to sit on the surface and ripen in the sun.

I start to sow about two rows of sets in late August; varieties like 'Autumn Queen' and 'Imai Yellow'. Come Boxing Day, I like to sow seed of some of the exhibition onions such as 'Kelsae' and 'Robinsons Mammoth Improved'. This year I am trying out some seed of Peter Fisk's own strain of onion. Peter is a keen vegetable exhibitor and shows in Suffolk, Norfolk, Cambridgeshire, Essex and in National Vegetable Society shows. I have judged his vegetables many times and he is an excellent show man. I prick out the onions in pots as soon as they are as big as a pin. The seedlings are kept growing in the greenhouse until the end of March and then moved to a cold frame (when the cold weather is over, we hope!) I plant them out into the onion bed at the end of April in rows 1ft apart with 1ft space from onion to onion. A row of parsley is planted in between the rows of onion to ward off the onionfly. I also give dressings of Benlate, according to instructions, to guard against rot and mildew. When the seedlings are growing nicely out of doors, they can be given a tonic of nitrogen in June, but only in showery weather. I also feed with Phostrogen as a liquid feed; my brother and I swear by Phostrogen, it's an excellent liquid feed and also available in tablet form.

Another way I have of feeding vegetables and flowers is to have a forty-gallon tank three-quarters filled with water, plus a sack filled with farmyard manure. I give it a good stir – you must not worry about the smell (that's part and parcel of life, after all!) It looks like the colour of old tea after it has been standing for a few hours and is just what the onions like, every ten days or so.

Onion sets are grown like the onion plants, but the sets must be covered, or the birds will pull the little bulblets out on top of the soil. Plant 1ft from row to row and 8in from bulblet to bulblet. I think that the birds sit and watch when you start to plant the garden; the sparrows are little devils for pulling onions out of the ground! They probably think the little plants make good nesting material (it's a good idea to cut off the small straw tops of bulblets as a way of limiting this theft).

With many gardeners it was – and still is – the custom to plant certain kinds of onion on the shortest day 21st December and to harvest them on the longest day (21st June).

Parsnips

What would Christmas be without roast parsnip? It was said of the parsnip that it gave good nourishment and was used at the time of Lent. This probably meant that the parsnip could be used in so many ways at that time of year when most other vegetables were nearly finished. Another useful feature of the parsnip is that it is happy to remain in the ground in frosty weather – in fact, frost will improve the flavour; it makes it sweeter. Gardeners in years gone by used to walk along the rows and shake the tops of the plants singing:

As long as my arm,
As thick as my wrist.

I recently had a telephone call from a Mr Barker of Mendlesham, Suffolk, asking if his parsnip was a record. He had just dug it from the garden and it measured 54in long. The record from *Garden News* is, however, 142¼in – but I still think that 54in is a fair length, especially as Mr Barker had made no special preparation of his soil. Now if you are just an amateur gardener and only need your parsnips for the roasting tin, you will not wish for them to be more than 12–18in long. They like the same conditions as carrots (no freshly-manured land) and they do best in a deep, light soil which has been deeply dug.

If you wish to grow the long-rooted type, you will have to prepare the soil making a hole with a crowbar and filling this with peat and sand, as for the carrot sowing. Parsnip is one vegetable for which you should always sow fresh seed. It is no good saving seed from year to year as it soon loses its ability to germinate. The traditional sowing time is late February or early March, but this is often when the soil is still wet and cold and I have sown much later, even in the middle of April, and still got good root crops. Another point is, the colder the soil, the more erratically the seed comes up. Sometimes germination takes five to six weeks. My rows are 1ft apart, planting seeds in drills ½in deep. When the seedlings are about 1½in high, I single them out to 6–8in apart, or more for larger parsnips.

Canker is the most serious disease, it looks like rust in the parsnip. There does not seem to be a cure, but you can grow a canker resistant variety like 'Avonresister' or 'Gladiator F1' (I can't speak too highly of this last-named variety; it has a very sweet flavour and on my medium-heavy ground it grows a treat). My brother takes my parsnips up just before Christmas, leaving them on top of the soil, close to the path, to get good frosts. Then we cover them with soil so that they are easy to pull out once the bad weather sets in.

Another use for parsnips in the country is for homemade wine. I have known many people to feel bad after drinking a glass of parsnip wine, especially if it is three or four years old.

Varieties are: 'Tender and True' (this is still the long variety used for exhibitions) and 'Hollow Crown Improved' (also the exhibitors' choice), 'Offenham', 'White Gem' and 'The Student'.

Peas

This vegetable makes me think of my mother, as she used to make a wonderful pea soup. When the family was coming in on a cold winter's day, the yellow mixing bowl would be on the table, full of soup with other vegetables mixed in and 'swimmers' (dumplings) floating on top. You needed no meat with this satisfying concoction. The pea is high in protein and years ago it was always eaten in Lent as you were forbidden to eat meat during that time. The Tudors used to eat only dried peas, but later they were used as a green vegetable. Tusser wrote:

Good Peason and Leeks to make Poredge in Lent,
And Peascods in July save Fish to be Spent,
Those having with other things plentifull then,
Thou winnest the Love of the Labouring Men.
(*Peason* – correct plural of Pea)

'Sow Beans or Peas on St. David's or St. Chad's
Be the weather good or bad'

With the small gardens of today not everyone has the space to grow peas. They take up a lot of room in proportion to the size of the crop, but with the hybrids, pods may be eaten as well as the peas, so I don't consider them a waste of room. I, for one, like the 'Asparagus Pea' or 'Winged Pea'; not only is it a nice vegetable, but it has a pretty red flower. The pods must be picked when they are about 1in long – if they are left to grow longer they become tough and stringy (the more you pick, the more they come).

Peas don't like heat, frost or drought. They do like a good rich soil but the risks are great with birds and mice. It helps to start growing under glass or frame. Heights vary from 18in to 6ft but most cottage gardens grow short varieties. The tall ones are mostly grown by the flower show exhibitor. You will find two sorts of seed; the smooth, round pea which is for early sowing and the wrinkled pea which is much sweeter and heavier cropping but not so hardy when growing.

Some troubles to be faced when growing peas are the pea moth (moths in the peas which turn to maggots) and pea mildew (a particular problem when dry weather occurs). Birds will pick off the tiny shoots as soon as they show out of the ground and the worst culprit of all is the jay – he just tears open the pods and eats the peas, leaving the pods hanging on the plant. Jays can be a real menace in the country; they are one of our prettiest birds, but they do so much damage.

There are dozens of varieties of pea to grow. First earlies are sometimes planted in late autumn and the best variety is 'Feltham First', but over the years a wrinkled pea has come in for early sowing and 'Hurst's Beagle' is very good. Two old favourites are 'Kelvedon Wonder' and 'Little Marvel'; all grow to around 18in high. I still put a few twigs near my peas; as they grow the twigs help to keep them from flopping about. Second earlies are 'Hurst Green Shaft' (this really is an outstanding pea; pods are often 5in long with up to eleven peas in a pod and this variety will grow to 3ft tall); 'Onward' (my father's favourite) and 'Trio' (this pea grows in bunches of three to four pods together, which makes it easier to pick). For a late cropper try 'Senator'. This one grows to 2½ft in height and is a good pea for small gardens. 'Mange-tout

Pea' (you can eat pea, pod and all) is being grown in many smaller gardens today. 'Sugar Snap' is a dual purpose pea. When young, it can be eaten like 'Mange-tout', then as it grows older, it can be stringed and eaten like dwarf beans. 'Oregon Sugar Pea' is one of the finest in this class of pea. Growing to 3ft high, it pods best if picked early so don't let pods get too big.

I like to sow my peas in drills about 2in deep in rows 1ft apart. I usually put peas in an old tin with some paraffin oil for about an hour, this should help to keep the mice away. Birds love the young shoots, so my brother protects the rows with black cotton or wire mesh guards to keep them off.

Potatoes

Potatoes have come a long way since they were introduced to this country by Sir Walter Raleigh. The potato took time to be accepted in Europe because – wait for it – once again this vegetable was supposed to be an aphrodisiac! (a potato an aphrodisiac? I don't believe it!) This vegetable was the main vegetable for poor families so perhaps this accounts for the large-size family! Years ago some people believed the potato to be poisonous. I expect this was because some of the tops of potatoes were eaten when growing.

Several of my radio listeners have asked me what those little green balls like tomatoes are which grow on potato tops. On no account must these be eaten as they are very poisonous indeed. A tuber left on top of the soil will soon turn green and bitter after being exposed to light and this also becomes poisonous. Now, after all that, you probably won't wish to grow the common 'spud'.

Good Friday was the traditional day for the countryman to plant his potatoes, after he had been to church. It was thought that the devil had no power over the soil on that day.

Plant your Potatoes when the Moon is on the Wane,
They want to grow down, that is plain.

Another old wives' tail is that potatoes should be dug-up after sunset, then they will not rot. Yet another yarn is that the local Scottish family should have the first potato or the crop would rot (but each member of the family must have a taste).

Another is to put a small potato in your pocket to relieve toothache. Farmers used to say that when the wagtail was about, it would be time to plant the potatoes (the wagtail was called 'potato setter'). In our day the potato is accepted as part of our daily diet. I think there is nothing nicer than that first root of new potatoes, cooked with green mint. I always freeze some of the early roots of tubers and put sprigs of mint in the bags when freezing. Potatoes take up a lot of room, so I don't expect small gardeners to grow them.

The seed tubers will appear in the shops after Christmas. Once you get the seed it will need 'chitting'. This means standing tubers up in old egg trays so that they can send out little shoots or eyes; this will give the tuber a head start when planting out, and you will get a much heavier yield. Do keep them out of the way of frost (avoid frost pockets or exposed ground). The best size for a seed potato is that of a pullet's (young chicken's) egg. My father's way of planting the common spud was in rows 2ft apart, putting a line across the garden and planting the potatoes 12–14in apart in the first trench, turning the soil over until coming to the next row, then putting the line across and starting again. My brother still plants my seed tubers in this way.

The soil cannot be too loose for potatoes and we find that trench planting is the most satisfactory method. If you are hoping to grow them for show work, lay dry leaves and peat round your seed tubers – grass cuttings put round the tubers also help to prevent 'scab'. Dig in compost, but don't lime before planting. Disease is only skin-deep so you can still eat the potatoes. The tubers are planted in March (these are first earlies). If you are on poor soil, a light dressing of soot will help (if you can find any nowadays). If there is a frost warning and potatoes are just coming through the soil, cover with old newspapers, old grass, even straw will do, or pull the soil back over the 'haulms'. Frost can blacken the tender young shoots and will set the plant back, with a few weeks growth lost. Also protect them by pulling compost over, otherwise they will turn green and become inedible.

The potato can suffer from many diseases, one of which is potato blight. A wet season will bring this on in July and August. You will notice brown patches on the leaves. Once the blight has taken hold on your plot there is no complete cure, but you can treat with Dithane, spraying every two weeks. This will help to stop the disease spreading. Wire worm is another pest, especially with new gardens, but this can be overcome by putting Bromophos in the soil before planting tubers.

Here are some varieties I like to grow but there are many others.
First early: – 'Arran Pilot', Maris Bard', 'Vanessa' (very good), 'Pentland Javelin'.
Second early: 'Wilja', 'Estima', 'Maris Peer'.
Maincrop: 'Majestic', 'Desiree', 'Pentland Crown', 'Drayton' (very good), 'Romano'.

Radish

The radish is a root vegetable which must be eaten young and tender to be appreciated. It is the easiest salad vegetable to cultivate and the quickest to germinate. If you can make a sowing every ten days or so until the end of July, you should have plenty of young radishes for salads throughout the season, but you must remember to thin out the plants from sowing, leaving them 1in apart. Another must is to water the seedlings as they are unable to withstand dry weather. Summer varieties suitable for forcing may be sown in midwinter in a cool greenhouse. I grow a lot of radishes because they are so useful for marking the rows of slower growing vegetables like parsnips, carrots and onions.
Varieties are 'Cherry Belle' (globe) – one of the best, 'French Breakfast' (long), 'Sparkler' (globe) and 'Prinz Rotin' (globe). Winter varieties are 'Black Spanish' (long) and 'China Rose'.

The turnip 'Tokio Cross' can be grown and eaten like a radish.

Sweetcorn

I think that maize, or corn as we call it must be the vegetable which has spread most widely around the world. Most countries now grow some variety or other. The sweetcorn grown in our gardens is simply maize which we pick before the grain is ripe. We then cook it and serve it with butter. Sweetcorn has become very fashionable in restaurants over the past few years, often served as a 'starter.'

Hot, sunny weather is needed to grow sweetcorn successfully. Plant in blocks to ensure pollination, spacing plants 15–18in apart. I always start my corn in peat pots, as this vegetable resents having its roots disturbed. Plant two seeds to a pot, 1in deep, then the weakest seedling can be pulled out. Harden plants off well before planting out and after the frosts are over. You may need to put some stakes in and tie the corn up if winds are a problem. Harvest the corn when tassels have turned brown at the top of the cob. Varieties are 'Earliglo (very good), 'First of All' (early, extra sweet), 'Polar Vee F1' (one of the earliest sweetcorn to produce cobs).

Sweetcorn is one vegetable which you should eat as soon as it has been picked; freshness is all-important for flavour.

Swede, Turnip and Kohlrabi

In the early part of this century, country people had little more than the swede and turnip to live on. Kohlrabi was used for sheep feeding, but it has become a popular vegetable today. The variety 'Rowel' is particularly good; the flesh is sweet and it is slow to turn woody. I think that the kholrabi is more popular on the Continent than in this country. A delicious vegetable, rather like the turnip, it can be eaten raw or cooked; the leaves can also be cooked like spinach. Kohlrabi has a globe-like root and grows on top of the soil. Pull them as soon as they get to the size of a tennis ball, as this is the best stage for them to be eaten. Sow seeds between April and June and thin out to 6in apart. Other varieties are 'White Vienna' and 'Purple Vienna'.

The swede is a good stand-by vegetable – what can be nicer than a dish of mashed swede with plenty of butter, salt and pepper, served with cold meat and pickles? Maybe I am old-fashioned, but I still think that you cannot grow a really good swede in the garden; those grown in the fields are much better in Suffolk and I am told that good field swedes are grown in Devon. However, I still have a go with a row or two and get some medium-sized roots. Like the kohlrabi and turnip, they belong to the Brassicae family so you have to watch out for club-root. Generally speaking, you don't get so much trouble with these root families as you tend to do with the leafy ones like cabbage etc.

The swede likes a firm soil and a sunny spot. Sow seeds thinly ½in deep with the rows 18in apart in early summer. Sowing any earlier will only see the seeds going to seed or they will be ready far too early; remember that the swede is a cold weather vegetable so it needs to be harvested in late October or November. I store the roots in the same way as carrots and beetroot; in boxes of old peat and sand. Varieties are 'Marian', 'Wilhelmsburger Gelbe' (the best I have grown) and 'Purple Top'.

I prefer eating turnips raw, rather than cooked (school dinners of cooked turnip and swede put us off them in our early years). French cooks like the turnip and I am told that they do some delicious dishes with this vegetable. I remember my father used to sow turnip seed all over the garden in late autumn, then he would dig in the tops when the turnip was about 4–5in high, using this as a green manure. People often shun turnips, regarding them as cattle and sheep feed. If you have a small garden, I would suggest growing just one row later in the summer for autumn harvesting, or an early row for eating like radish ('Tokio Cross'). Turnips and swedes don't transplant very well, so the art is to sow thinly where they are to grow. You can eat the tops of the turnips when they are 4in high; they are stored like swedes.

Flea beetle can be a problem when growing turnips, so dust with a derris dust – you will soon notice that the leaves will get small holes in them. Varieties are : Early – 'Gilfeather', 'Snowball', 'Tokio Cross', 'Purple Top' and 'Milan'. Maincrop – 'Golden Ball', 'Green Top' and 'White'.

Tomato

Old herbalists used to call tomatoes 'apples of love'. This versatile vegetable is in ever-increasing demand and most gardeners, in both small and large gardens, grow tomatoes in some form. At one time they were always grown under glass, but with modern hybrids you can have a choice of variety as there are literally dozens to take your fancy. They usually form some part of our daily diet today. Years ago the fruits of the tomato were considered harmful and even poisonous. The first seed came from Peru, and if you didn't know, the tomato is a relative of the potato family. If you get potato blight, the disease can also be passed on to tomatoes when spores are blown into the greenhouse, so watch out!

You will have to treat this vegetable in a rather special manner if you are short of space; it doesn't like frost or very hot weather. If you just need to grow a few plants outside, they will need less attention than the greenhouse varieties. Years ago, tomato seed was sown at full moon. Another old wives' tale was that the tomato was happiest if planted near asparagus – and garlic should also be planted nearby to keep diseases at bay. Even stinging-nettles were supposed to make the plants grow well. With the aid of grow-bags the smallest balcony can grow one or two plants, as well as wee ones in a flower pot on the windowsill in the kitchen, such as 'Tiny Tim' and 'Minibel'.

I feel that there are three ways to grow tomatoes in the greenhouse; in pots or ring culture, in grow-bags, or straight into the soil of the greenhouse border. One point to remember is not to sow your seed too early. If you do, the plants will come up and often turn bluey-grey if not kept at the right temperature and the seedlings never seem to recover from the cold with the inevitable result that the plants are checked. Sow the seed in trays, sowing thinly, and cover with compost, keeping at a temperature of 65°F. When the first leaf appears, prick out into 3in pots. Transplant your seedlings into their permanent positions when the first flower appears, about 6–9in high. If you are planting the tomatoes in the borders of your greenhouse, the soil must be prepared. Dig in plenty of good farmyard manure, as tomatoes are gross feeders. Plant them 18in apart – if you plant too close, this will reduce air circulation and can create growth problems. Also try to stagger plants if you are growing two rows, and give a good watering. You may wish to grow a few plants in grow-bags. The compost in the bags has all the correct food added, but as the bags warm-up quickly they will need more water. Support the plants with string and stakes. I put my stakes in when I dig the holes for the plants so that the roots are not disturbed.

The next thing to worry about is side-shooting. This refers to the little side shoots which grow in what we call the leaf axils, where the leaf joins the stem. If you don't do this little job, your tomatoes will be growing like tryffids (rum old plants). Pinch out the tops of the tomatoes when there are seven or eight trusses on the plant. Start feeding throughout their period of growth. Once the trusses have formed, in order to get a good pollination, tap the stakes first thing in the morning to release the small clouds of pollen.

If the greenhouse gets very hot, do put some shading on the glass as the plants do not like very hot weather. Bush tomatoes grown outside will not need side shoots pinched out but, like the greenhouse variety, they need plenty of good compost and watering.

The main pest with tomatoes grown in the greenhouse is whitefly. I grow dwarf African marigolds amongst the tomatoes as this does help to keep the fly down. Varieties are: Greenhouse – 'Shirley' (very good), 'Curabel', 'Moneymaker', 'Ultura Boy', 'Tigerella', 'Red Ensign', 'Alicante' and 'Supercross'.
Outdoor – 'Red Alert', 'The Amateur', 'Alfresco', 'Outdoor Girl', 'Sweet 100' and 'Gardeners Delight'.

Remember to put one red tomato in a tray of green ones at the end of the season, or a red apple, as the gas from the red fruit, called 'ethyl', will help to ripen the fruit.

Gardening Snippets

How to make a compost

The compost heap is a must for any garden. Many years ago, my grandfather (and later my dad) had a big hole at the top of the garden where they used to put all their rubbish. A pail stood outside the back door and all the household 'chates' (tea leaves, vegetable peelings etc) were put into this, all to be saved for the compost heap. Nowadays a compost heap is made in layers, all very modern and proper. We have ours in between two sheds, with old corrugated tin made up into a box shape, 4ft x 3ft. All our garden waste plus the household chates are put into this container.

The correct way to make a compost heap is to start at ground level. You need surrounding space to let in air, an area of about 7ft x 3ft. Put all waste vegetable matter into your compost container in the form of a layer; such as weeds, cabbage leaves, pea haulms, soft hedge clippings and lawn mowings, in fact, any soft green stuff that will rot down. Don't put old cabbage stalks in as they take so long to rot (we stand ours up to dry, then have a good bonfire and burn them). Be careful not to put any diseased material in your compost as this will only spread disease all over the garden. When you have a good green layer, about 4in high, sprinkle manure, if possible, on to the heap (we put chicken-droppings on ours). If no manure is available, sprinkle the heap with sulphate of ammonia at the rate of ½oz to the square yard, then sprinkle the heap with 8 gallons of water. There are also proprietary products on the market today; if you went to a garden centre and said that you were going to make a compost heap, they would, I am sure tell you what to use. You could then use a special product instead of the sulphate of ammonia. Carry on in this way with the layers at a rate of 4oz chalk or lime to a square yard; this all helps to break down the compost and sweeten it. When the compost is about 4ft high, start another heap. If the weather turns very hot give the mixture a good watering each week, and turn the heap every six weeks. In years gone by, my husband Ernie and I didn't use any chemicals on our compost, we just let the rubbish rot down of its own free will, then we used most of it for our runner bean trench. It is surprising how much you need for just this purpose. If only people realised how much they could plough back into the soil, what a benefit it would be to the garden. Even old newspaper rots down if you tear it up into little shreds. You don't see many people doing that nowadays, but during the war when we were all 'digging for victory', it was quite a common practice.

Flowers to Eat?

Have you ever thought of having flowers on the menu? Disraeli loved the primrose, not just for its good looks, but for its flavour. He liked the young shoots soaked in salt water for a few minutes, drained and boiled for ten minutes, then dressed in a vinaigrette sauce and decorated with the flowers. The use of flowers in cooking is age-old. Roots, stems, leaves and petals have always been valued, not just for decoration but to impart an individual aroma or flavour, or to give the dish some medicinal quality. Alas, flower eating is a taste which has all but disappeared in the West, but is still widely practised in the varying cuisines of the Orient.

The Chinese have a proverb; if you have two loaves of bread, sell one and buy a lily. They are far too practical a people to live in a land where flowers grow freely and not make use of them. The lotus, for example, was, and still is, both beautiful and nourishing; every part of this exotic plant is used by the Chinese cook. The tuber is eaten as a vegetable or sliced and candied. The stems are stuffed with pork, onions and fresh root ginger mixed with soya sauce and corn starch, dipped in batter and fried, then served hot. The seeds are candied for the Chinese New Year and the flowers enhance the flavour and appearance of steaming bowls of rice.

Another warming and delicious Chinese dish is a salad made from hollyhocks. The young buds and flowers are gathered, tossed in a garlic-free dressing and served in delicate porcelain bowls. Later in the year, they use chrysanthemums in the same way. A word of warning – if you decide next summer that you would like to try hollyhock salad, do bear in mind that this flower was once used as a laxative.

Indians cooked and ate flowers they had strewn upon the altars of their gods. The tiger lily was grown in ancient Mexican gardens for its stately beauty, its chestnut flavour and ability to allay hunger. Marigold adds a burst of gold to many otherwise dull dishes. The Dutch broths in the Middle Ages were considered incomplete without the addition of this flower's golden petals. Medieval French and English cooks liked the piquant flavour fresh and dried marigolds gave to their sweet dishes. Try adding a cupful of bruised marigold petals to homemade custard, with nutmeg and allspice, and serve either on it's own or with a dash of rosewater, decorated with whipped cream and marigold petals. Or, what about marigold sandwiches? Wedge thin slices of cheese and liverwurst with marigold petals and mayonnaise, sprinkled with toasted sesame seeds, between two slices of wholemeal bread.

Bees in the Garden

A swarm of bees cannot be turned
A dead bee makes no money.
Bees have honey in their mouths but stings in their tails.

When bees are old they yield no honey.

A swarm of bees in May is worth a load of hay,
A swarm of bees in June is worth a silver spoon.
A swarm of bees in July isn't worth a fly.

Gardeners cannot do without bees. Two important points to be kept in mind are that a garden should be in full sunlight and not shaded by trees or buildings, and that plants should be grown in bold groups. More and more people (especially gardeners) are going in for bee-keeping. I was always told by my father that in days gone by most cottages had a hive of bees and when anybody in the family died, one had to lay a piece of black cloth on the hive and tell the bees who was dead, otherwise it would bring bad luck to the family. I still don't like to see bees come indoors – there are so many sad tales told about them coming in the house. Bumble bees are also said to bring bad luck to the household.

The flowers of a number of everyday vegetables are attractive to bees for nectar and pollen. Where seed production takes place on a large scale they may be of appreciable monetary value. Vegetables which flower during their normal life-span and which attract bees are marrows, pumpkins and the bean family. I love to see the bees on broad beans. Sometimes I have known runner beans to be sprayed with sugar and water to get the bees to help make the flowers set, to produce the beans.

Flowers which encourage bees to the garden are as follows:

Alyssum	Alliums	Anchusa
Lemon Balm	Aster	Borage
Candytuft	Erigeron	Clary
Clarkia	Centaurea	Cheiranthus (Siberian Wallflower)
Dahlia (Coltness Single mixed)	Limnanthes (douglasii)	Godetia
Lavatera	Lunaria (Honestry)	
Linum (Flax)	Mignonette	Malope (Mallow)
Marjoram	Phacelia	Myosotis (Forget-me-not)
Poppy	Heather (all types)	
Wallflower		Sunflower

These are just a few suitable flowers and herbs. There are many more, but the list I have given will help if you are thinking of keeping a hive of bees in your garden.

I marvel at how bees work! They must fly miles and miles to collect pollen for making honey. Sometimes they make their homes in old hollows of trees, and even in the roof of a house if they can find a hole to get inside. So it is not just a matter of having a hive in the garden. An average colony of bees depends on 60,000 workers, so I am told, with one queen bee, and they make well over

400lb of honey, using about a third for their own consumption.

The life of the honey bee is short, sometimes only six months or so, but the queen bee can live for four to five years. A colony consists of three different types of bee – the queen, worker and drone. The queen bee is the only fertilised female and lives in the hive to lay eggs. The drones are males which help to maintain the hive temperature and provide the initial fertilisation of the queen. Towards the end of the summer they are driven off by the workers, to die. All bees depend on flowers for food, the female bees feeding on nectar from plants, collecting the surplus in a compartment of their stomachs. On reaching the hive, they regurgitate the surplus and make this into honey. Flowers depend on bees as much as the bees depend on flowers.

Bees will only sting if provoked. However, a bee sting remedy is to rub a bruised leaf of summer savory on the sting and it will help to ease the affected part – the common dock leaf will also bring relief.

Peggy's Patch Gardening Tips

From Mrs Violet Thompson, Great Waltham

When planting seed potatoes, if you are one short for a row, take a potato with good eyes, cut it in half with a sharp knife and rub the halves with dry dirt to seal them.

From Mrs V. J. Vale, Marlesford, Woodbridge

A large, 2 litre lemonade bottle (the plastic type with a black base) will, when empty, make an ideal shield around tender plants and is also slug and snail-proof if left with the lid on, but pierced with holes for air. Cut the bottle off level at the black base and also at the top, if needed. Remove the central clear plastic piece from the black base and it will make an ideal, small flower pot. With its slightly raised centre and drilled with a few small holes, this hardy, little homemade pot will not get waterlogged.

From Mrs M. Simmonds, Sudbury

Carrots can be started effectively in old toilet-roll and kitchen-roll centres. Fill the cardboard cylinders with compost, set two or three seeds in each and stand in a box in your shed until they start to grow. When the seedlings are a suitable size for planting-out, set the entire 'package' in the ground – the holder will simply rot away.

Use a plastic lemonade bottle as a watering vessel indoors and out – make holes in the cap and you can then squeeze the bottle.

Use an old pair of tights, cut up, for drainage in pots.

From Mr B. Rose, Rushmere, Ipswich

Pests in cabbage plants can be kept at bay like this: take a dozen mothballs, crush them into a gallon bucket with a little hot water, top up with cold water and sprinkle around the roots. Old-fashioned mothballs contain napthalene and this chemical can be used to combat cabbage root and carrot fly.

From 'Betty', East Bergholt

A useful and cheap tip for keeping slugs off delicate plants such as lettuce and other seedlings without harming birds or other family pets: collect and dry eggshells and crush them into smallish pieces. These can be kept in a plastic bag or empty jar until required. Put a good border of crushed eggshells around the plants when you plant out and they will keep slugs away.

'Peggy's Patch' is broadcast on *The Allan Lee Programme* every Wednesday at 11.00 am on Radio Orwell (257m MW 97.1 FM Stereo) and on Saxon Radio (240m MW 96.4 FM Stereo). And *Gardening Hour* on Fridays at 6-30 – 7-30pm.

Index